Walter Lynwood Fleming Lectures in Southern History
LOUISIANA STATE UNIVERSITY

GAVIN WRIGHT

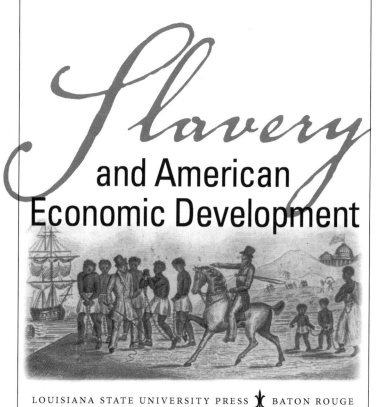

Slavery and American Economic Development

LOUISIANA STATE UNIVERSITY PRESS ✸ BATON ROUGE

Published by Louisiana State University Press
Copyright © 2006 by Louisiana State University Press
All rights reserved
Manufactured in the United States of America
Louisiana Paperback Edition, 2013

Designer: Barbara Neely Bourgoyne
Typeface: Adobe Minion Pro, text; Univers, display

Library of Congress Cataloging-in-Publication Data

Wright, Gavin.
  Slavery and American economic development / Gavin Wright.
    p. cm. — (Walter Lynwood Fleming lectures in southern history)
  Includes bibliographical references and index.
    1. Slavery—Economic aspects—United States. 2. United States —
  Economic conditions—To 1865. 3. Right of property—United States—
  History.   I. Title. II. Series.
  E441.W83 2007
  306.3'620973—dc22

                                              2006002038

ISBN 978-0-8071-5228-7 (pbk: alk. paper) — ISBN 978-0-8071-5275-1 (pdf) —
    ISBN 978-0-8071-5276-8 (epub) — ISBN 978-0-8071-5277-5 (mobi)

The paper in this book meets the guidelines for permanence
and durability of the Committee on Production Guidelines for
Book Longevity of the Council on Library Resources.
∞

To the memory of
BILL PARKER
(1919–2000)
and
BOB GALLMAN
(1926–1998)

CONTENTS

PREFACE

These essays were first presented as the Fleming Lectures at Louisiana State University in April 1997. My only excuse for the long lag between oral delivery and printed publication is that I wanted time to flesh out the supporting evidence, update the coverage of the academic literature, and work through the argument with some care to make it accessible to a general readership. Inevitably these tasks take longer than expected. But my opportunity finally arrived with a sabbatical at the Stanford Humanities Center during 2003–4. I am grateful to the center for providing an ideal working environment for completing the revision.

Although extensively revised, with an introduction and epilogue now added, the structure of the essays and the main themes are essentially the same as presented in 1997. They represent an effort at reframing several debates relating to the economics of slavery, emphasizing the economic concept of property rights, and the historical context of the onset of modern economic development in Europe and North America between the eighteenth and nineteenth centuries. To some extent the larger point is methodological, but the essays do not shrink from advancing strong positions on major historical issues. Readers may now judge their persuasiveness for themselves.

Because the essays are a distillation of ideas that have evolved over many years, it would be impossible to list all of those whose contributions have influenced the end result in one way or another. But for specific advice on early drafts of these essays, I would like to thank Robin Blackburn, Paul Rhode, Alan Olmstead, and an anonymous reader for Louisiana State University Press. For research assistance, I thank Daniel Rubens, whose 2005 Stanford Honors thesis has informed and enriched my account of the slavery debate in the Old Northwest.

Chapter 3 draws upon material first published in *Agricultural History* in 2003 (previously appearing as "Slavery and American Agriculture," *Agricultural History* 77 (2003): 527–52; copyright © 2003 by the American History Society). I am grateful to the University of California Press for permission to use this material here.

Special thanks go to LSU Press for its patience, and to Rand Dotson for facilitating publication. I am especially grateful to Mary Lee Eggart of the LSU Department of Geography and Anthropology for her expert assistance with the maps and figures.

My warmest appreciation is to the history community at LSU, whose invitation supplied the spark that has now culminated in this book. My wife, Cathe, and I retain fond memories of the courteous welcome and hospitality provided by then-chair Paul F. Paskoff and his colleagues. We are also grateful to legal historian Richard Kilbourne Jr., who introduced one of the lectures and shared with us his rich knowledge of Louisiana history. My main regret at the long delay in publication is that the book will not get a response from Carville Earle, the distinguished LSU historical geographer, who died in 2003. Carville and I did not always agree on the relationship between slavery and American geography, but I always respected his expertise and benefited from his penetrating questions, several of which he raised during our conversations at the time of the lectures. As always, this book would not have been completed without Cathe's love and support. She has my eternal gratitude.

Slavery and American Economic Development

What Was Slavery?

When Abraham Lincoln said, "if slavery is not wrong, then nothing is wrong," he neatly epitomized the tendency to think of slavery as an absolute category, a standard by which all other evils are overshadowed. This conception, often implicit, has a powerful hold on Americans down to the present day. It infuses most writing in American history, even in an age with little sympathy or respect for any number of other long-entrenched orthodoxies. To be sure, the hegemony of antislavery thinking does not stop the occasional flirtation with relativism, using arguments familiar to antebellum apologists: slaves had no risk of unemployment or starvation, there were many other forms of unfreedom in earlier times, and material conditions among slaves in the United States were relatively favorable, as reflected in high rates of population growth. But such unthinkable thoughts gain attention mainly because they are shocking. When moral issues are raised, the evil of slavery is taken as axiomatic. The resulting shallowness of thought was well described at a session of the Southern Historical Association, when Barbara Fields observed that few of her students could "last two minutes in the ring" against the most mediocre proslavery apologists from the Old South.

Don't worry. It is not the purpose of these essays to reopen the antebellum debate over the morality of slavery. There is, however, a parallel problem in economics and economic history, namely the impulse to identify properties of "slavery" as an organizational form or system of production, as though that term stood for a clearly defined, well-understood economic arrangement, to be contrasted with "free" or "wage" labor. The aim of this book is to restructure the discussion on the economic history of slavery by unpacking these conventional categories and examining their constituent elements. That which we call slavery was not the same economic species in all historical times and places, and even less did free labor represent a specific, well-defined alternative. Assessing the place of the peculiar institution in American economic development calls for a clear specification of how exactly slavery was peculiar.

This is a tall order. The task is reduced somewhat by a primary focus on mainland North America and, ultimately, the United States. But the interpretation draws upon the rich literature that has emerged in recent decades on slavery, the slave trade, and the rise of the Atlantic economy during what we Americans call the colonial era, and this intellectual strategy entails certain risks. Slavery on the North American mainland had many distinctive features, the most obvious of which was demographic: the strong positive rate of natural increase of the slave population, which in turn generated an interest in accumulating wealth in the form of slaves, a motivation that permeated political as well as economic behavior. It is difficult to find counterparts to this behavioral configuration elsewhere in the Americas. But this and a host of other differences need not be fatal to comparative studies, if some of the underlying principles were the same, and this is the case that I put before my readers in the essays that follow.

The core of the proposed restructuring is to distinguish three dimensions or aspects to slavery: (1) slavery as a form of labor relations, (2) slavery as a set of property rights, and (3) slavery as a political regime.

DIMENSIONS OF SLAVERY

Adam Smith argued that because a slave could not own property he "can have no other interest but to eat as much, and to labour as little as possible. Whatever work he does beyond what is sufficient to purchase his own maintenance, can be squeezed out of him by violence only . . ." Smith's sharp condemnation of slavery became extremely influential, but as Seymour Drescher has noted, his assertion about the inefficiency of slave labor was commonplace in eighteenth-century Britain. Nor did

Smith's analysis of the institution rise to his normal scientific standard. He identified the slaveowner's motive in perpetuating such brutality as "the pride of man" that "makes him love to domineer," and slavery persisted only where crops were sufficiently profitable to "afford the expence of slave-cultivation." Although elsewhere Smith was careful to analyze the interaction between individual motives and social outcomes, when it came to slavery he did not even ask how such self-indulgent enterprises could survive in a competitive world. In light of the gap between the decisiveness of Smith's conclusion and the flimsiness of his analysis, it is perhaps not surprising that the next two generations of economic theorists fell "almost completely silent" on the question of the comparative performance of slave versus free labor.[1]

Nonetheless, the belief in slavery's inefficiency on motivational grounds has persisted. Because their chief concern was slavery's inhumanity, abolitionist critics emphasized the human element in the situation, the hopelessness of the slave's position and therefore the lack of incentive for physical exertion. Among American abolitionists, the assumption that slave labor was unproductive because the lash was an ineffective incentive was largely unquestioned. Primarily through introspection rather than direct observation, they focused on problems of *production*, on slavery as a *form of labor relations*. This tradition was subsequently handed down by historians of diverse schools of thought. In his scathing indictment of slavery and British capitalism—which actually had little to do with slavery as a system of production—Eric Williams wrote in 1944: "Slave labor is given reluctantly; it is unskilful, it lacks versatility." In the 1950s, Kenneth Stampp wrote that "slavery was above all a labor system," in which "masters measured the success of their methods by the extent to which their interest in a maximum of work of good quality prevailed over the slaves' predilection for a minimum of work of indifferent quality." And in the 1960s, Eugene Genovese's chapter on "The Low Productivity of Southern Slave Labor" struck similar themes, noting that the arguments were virtually unchanged from those of contemporaries: "Bondage forced the Negro to give his labor grudgingly and badly, and his poor work habits

1. Smith, *Wealth of Nations*, vol. 1, 411–12; Drescher, *Capitalism and Antislavery*, 133; Drescher, *Mighty Experiment*, 55.

retarded those social and economic advances that could have raised the general level of productivity . . . Most competent observers agreed that slaves worked badly, without interest or effort."[2]

Not only was slave labor grudging and minimal in this view, but it was lacking in versatility and skill, and therefore limited the slave economy's potential for advancement. Thus Frederick Law Olmsted's northern readers would not have been surprised by the views of the Virginia slaveholder who held that "the negro could never be trained to exercise judgment; he cannot be made to use his mind; he always depends on machinery doing its own work, and cannot be made to watch it . . . It always seems on the plantation as if they took pains to break all the tools and spoil all the cattle that they possibly can, even when they know they'll be directly punished for it." Genovese maintained this tradition when he wrote: "The most obvious obstacle to the employment of better equipment was the slave himself . . . The harsh treatment that slaves gave equipment shocked travelers and other contemporaries, and neglect of tools figures prominently among the reasons given for punishing Negroes." A model proposed by Stefano Fenoaltea is a variation on this old story: the "pain incentives" of slavery were effective in "effort-intensive" activities like mining and plantation agriculture, but reward systems became superior in more advanced sectors where the required actions were "care-intensive."[3]

Robert Fogel's emphasis on the efficiency of slave labor may thus be seen as a response to a very old interpretation, turning it upside down. Although denying that slave labor was necessarily lacking in skill and versatility, Fogel argues that the geographic spread of slavery in the New World was firmly rooted in economies of scale derived from the use of gang labor methods on large plantations. These methods, which were only effective in a handful of staple crops, established a division of labor and a work routine that succeeded in "subjugating slaves to the regime of regu-

---

2. Williams, *Capitalism and Slavery*, 6; Stampp, *Peculiar Institution*, 34, 54; Genovese, *Political Economy of Slavery*, 43–44. On the views of American abolitionists, see Glickstein, "Poverty Is Not Slavery," 205.

3. Olmsted, *Slave States*, 85–86 (originally published as *Journey in the Seaboard Slave States* in 1856); Genovese, *Political Economy of Slavery*, 54–55; Fenoaltea, "Slavery and Supervision."

larity, transforming them into metaphoric clock punchers." "The principal function of the gang system was to speed up the pace of labor, to increase the intensity per hour." "The gang system played a role comparable to the factory system or, at a later date, the assembly line, in regulating the pace of labor. It was, in other words, a speedup." The persistence of beliefs to the contrary, according to Fogel, simply reflects the "assumption that productivity is necessarily virtuous," an attitude descended from the abolitionists who "refused to admit that the gang system could be technically more efficient than the free labor system."[4]

We now have a sufficient number of observations, however, to know that an extremely wide variety of labor relationships were possible under the name "slavery." That term does not define a single well-defined labor system any more than "free labor" usefully describes the full range of nonslave labor relationships in the world. Some slave systems extracted effort "by violence only," but we now know that the detailed labor arrangements on New World plantations were extremely diverse, from centralized gangs to individual task systems approximating piecework. The very term "sharecropper" originated in the turpentine forests of North Carolina in the 1830s, where predominantly slave laborers were assigned tasks in sections marked off into grids or "crops."[5] The literature on "informal contracts" and "collective labor bargaining" under slavery has flourished in recent years, demonstrating that labor relations had an evolutionary character under slavery just as they did under free-labor arrangements, and in both cases it is difficult to generalize about the outcomes. Ira Berlin and Philip D. Morgan summarize this research as follows: "The conflict between master and slave took many forms, involving the organization of labor, the pace of work, the division of labor, and the composition of the labor force—all questions familiar to students of wage labor . . . Through continuous struggle and endless

4. Fogel, *Without Consent or Contract*, 26, 78, 162, 409–11. The "speedup" quote is from Fogel, *Without Consent or Contract: Evidence and Methods*, 34. Fogel reaffirms his efficiency analysis in *Slavery Debates*, 29–44.

5. Morgan, "Task and Gang Systems"; Coclanis, "How the Low Country Was Taken to Task"; Outland, "Slavery, Work, and the Geography of the North Carolina Naval Stores Industry."

negotiation, both masters and slaves conceded what neither could alter, and, in time, both grudgingly agreed to what was acceptable, what might be tolerated, and what was utterly beyond endurance."[6]

Without denying the reality and importance of labor systems, it is appropriate to note that work organization *per se* was only one of the dimensions that distinguished slavery from alternatives. Broadly speaking, we can group these under two general headings: slavery as a set of property rights and slavery as a political regime. The first refers to the considerations that arose because slaves constituted legal property, a form of wealth and a basis for credit and exchange. Owners were entitled to do many things with their slave property that could not legally be done with free labor. From the earliest formulation in the 1661 slave code of Barbados, slaves were classified as property in the British colonies, bringing into play the weight of the common-law conceptions of property as they had evolved for nonhuman possessions over centuries. Fitting slavery into the system of Anglo-American common law was the central thrust of jurisprudence regarding slavery in both colonial and antebellum eras.[7]

To be sure, the laws of slavery varied over time and between one jurisdiction and another. David Galenson points out that one of the developments facilitating the transition from indentured servitude to slavery in the Chesapeake region was a clarification of property rights by the courts and the legislature. In contrast to servants, slaves did not have the right to sue their masters, and baptism of the mother did not change the legal status of her offspring. In the eighteenth century, the legal status of slaves as property became even more sharply defined in the British colonies. Jacob Price notes the role of the Colonial Debts Act of 1732 in the development of the British slave colonies, because it gave effective legal (and therefore

6. Berlin and Morgan, eds., *Cultivation and Culture*, 2, 6. Other studies in this subject area include Berlin and Morgan, eds., *Slaves' Economy*; Betty Wood, *Women's Work, Men's Work*; Mary Turner, ed., *From Chattel Slaves to Wage Slaves*. It should also be noted that Eugene Genovese's later work portrayed a far more nuanced and interactive labor relationship between master and slave than that suggested by the quotations cited above. See Genovese, *Roll, Jordan, Roll*, 292–317.

7. Finkelman, "Centrality of Slavery," 14–16; Higgenbotham and Kopytoff, "Property First, Humanity Second," 513–14; Hoffer, *Great New York Conspiracy*, 17–18; Morris, *Southern Slavery and the Law*, 2, 42, 61–62.

negotiable) status to the bonds given by planters buying slaves on credit. This was in contrast to the "Latin model," which emphasized protection of the plantation as a working unit.[8]

As important as such variations in the law undoubtedly were, over most of the era of modern slavery certain distinguishing legal features were persistent: Slaves could be purchased and carried to any location where slavery was legal; they could be assigned to any task—male or female, young or old; they could be punished for disobedience, with no effective recourse to the law; they could be accumulated as a form of wealth; they could be sold or bequeathed. Particularly in the British colonies, and subsequently in the United States, slaves could be used as the basis for credit transactions. Many of the property rights of slaveowners are conveniently summarized in the statement that slaves were chattels or personal property, a precept that prevailed at most times and in most places in North America. There were occasional exceptions, such as colonial Virginia (where slaves were considered real property between 1705 and 1792) and Louisiana (where the civil-law tradition classified slave property as real). But Thomas Morris's exhaustive survey of these variations concludes that the treatment of slaves as realty pertained only to a limited set of inheritance issues and by no means attached slaves to plantations, raised the status of slaves, nor preserved family units. The clear legal trend in the nineteenth century was toward full alienability of slave property in the market.[9]

These legal aspects of slavery and their economic implications, I contend, are where we should look in trying to understand the place of slavery in American economic development. They are more enduring and pervasive—more robust in the parlance of economics—than the particularities of work organizations and systems of discipline.

All such rights of slaveowners must be qualified, however, by considerations arising under the third aspect: slavery as a political regime. Rights mean little unless they are enforceable, and because slaves were held in captivity, slavery required a police system to prevent escape and to defend against revolt. Typically slave systems were also regimes of

8. Galenson, "Economic Aspects of the Growth of Slavery"; Price, "Credit in the Slave Trade."

9. Morris, *Southern Slavery and the Law,* 63–80.

racial subordination, requiring explicit hierarchies of racial categories and statuses. Many of the major issues about the compatibility between slavery and modern economic development fall into this third category. Every slave regime was vulnerable to rapid disintegration, no matter how successful its economic performance may have been, either by violent overthrow, as in St. Domingue, or by breakdown of the policing systems to prevent or deter running away. This was the nub of Stephen A. Douglas's reply to Abraham Lincoln's challenge known as the "Freeport question," whether the people of a territory had any lawful way to exclude slavery in the wake of the *Dred Scott* decision: ". . . the people have the lawful means to introduce it or exclude it as they please, for the reason that slavery cannot exist a day or an hour anywhere, unless it is supported by local police regulations . . . Those police regulations can only be established by the local legislature, and if the people are opposed to slavery they will elect representatives to that body who will by unfriendly legislation effectually prevent the introduction of it into their midst."[10] Douglas may have been on the wrong side of history in these debates, but on this point he was correct.

Choices that were profit-enhancing from the perspective of individual slaveowners were not necessarily optimal from the standpoint of preserving the system, a reflection of the standard economic distinction between individual incentives and collective or class interests. Thus, manumissions were prohibited or restricted in most slave states, not to enhance the *private* interests of individual owners, but to serve the *collective* interest of owners as a group, in the plausible belief that freedom for some would undermine the status of slavery for the rest. Elizabeth Fox-Genovese and Eugene Genovese write: "White southerners would have been mad to teach significant numbers of their slaves to read and write, to permit abolitionist literature to fall into their hands, to take an easy view of politicians, clergymen and editors who so much as questioned the morality and justice of the very foundation of their social order and domestic peace."[11] Such statements presume a collective or class perspective. The problems they pose for economic performance are not resolved through

10. Angle, ed., *Created Equal?* 152.
11. Fox-Genovese and Genovese, *Fruits of Merchant Capital,* 400–401.

micromodels of incentives and performance in production. Therefore, in addition to analyzing the implications of property rights in human beings for patterns of migration, trade, investment, and skill development—the subject matter conventionally assigned to microeconomics—we also have to consider the "politics of slavery" and its implications for economic development.

INTERDEPENDENCIES

The proposed three aspects of slavery are not always easy to distinguish, nor were they independent of each other as a matter of history. The legal rights of slaveowners certainly shaped and constrained systems of work. In James Oakes's succinct summary: "Slaves could be whipped, but they could not be fired; they could be bribed but not paid wages; they could be sold but not laid off; rewarded but not freed."[12] (Note that the last point appeals to a legal constraint, not necessarily an inherent feature of slavery, but one that prevailed as a practical matter in nineteenth-century America.) True enough, but neither economic theory nor empirical evidence from labor economics supports a presumption in favor of one system over another as a means of eliciting effective labor effort. Long-term labor attachments can be highly productive, but they can also settle into low-level bilateral bargaining traps, in which slaves "could mount collective resistance more easily and, in the short run, effectively, to proprietary initiatives than could free workers." Property rights allowed owners to capture the returns to investments in slave skills, but possession of skills gave the slaves added leverage when it came to specifics. According to one study of slave ironworkers, the owner and his managers "were apparently willing to tolerate a certain amount of neglect of duty in order to avoid difficulty with key black personnel."[13]

How should we classify the hours of labor, so often an object of struggle both in the workplace and through political channels? Unquestionably, one of the privileges of slave ownership was the right to specify

12. Oakes, *Slavery and Freedom*, 54.

13. The first quote is from John Bezís-Selfa, "A Tale of Two Ironworks," 700. The second is from Charles B. Dew, "Disciplining Slave Ironworkers," 412.

hours of work, and slaves had no legal right to object. When Chesapeake tobacco plantations switched from predominantly servant to predominantly slave labor after 1690, Lorena Walsh reports that the number of workdays increased to include a full Saturday, and these workdays were often extended into work at night, beating corn into meal with mortars and pestles. Even Sundays were not inviolate. Yet we also know that such requirements could become objects of (perhaps implicit) bargaining, so that "with time, slave owners found it prudent to compensate for Sunday work with food or a little cash." Ultimately free Sundays came to be seen as an entitlement, as slaves perfected techniques to "foil their owners' demands and expand control over their own labor and lives."[14] Thus the sharp distinction sometimes proposed between hours of labor and the intensity of labor does not closely track the historical record as a distinctive feature of slavery.

The purpose of distinguishing labor relations from property rights is not to establish an airtight set of categories but to redirect attention from the human drama of slavery at the microlevel to the larger systemic features of slavery that gave the institution its distinctive place in American economic history. Although the emphasis on labor relations is entirely understandable and appropriate for those trying to recover the human experience of slavery, the contention of these essays is that the latter category has been underappreciated relative to the former, if our objective is to understand the relationship between slavery and American economic development. Thus, in the larger sweep of economic history, the struggle over hours and working conditions was less vital than the capacity of the slaveowner to override prevailing cultural norms regarding the division of labor within the household—for example, by assigning female slaves to field work during seasons of peak labor demand—an effect that I place firmly under the "property rights" heading. Chapter 1 argues that the central role for slavery in the rise of the eighteenth-century Atlantic economy is attributable to property rights rather than efficiency advantages of slavery in production.

To be sure, the enforcement issue was potentially even more vital for the viability of slavery, as became evident during wartime settings. The

14. Walsh, "Slave Life, Slave Society," 174–77; Berlin, *Many Thousands Gone*, 117–34.

violent revolution in St. Domingue is unique in the Western Hemisphere, but it nonetheless illustrates a more common pattern whereby wars that were initially unrelated to slavery (the French Revolution in this case) generated an atmosphere that undermined the political authority of slave-owners. When the Union army marched through the South in the late stages of the Civil War, the troops were often greeted by crowds of slaves who had walked off the plantations, correctly perceiving that their unfree status was no longer enforceable. "Whenever northern soldiers appeared," writes Armstead Robinson, "their presence struck the 'peculiar institution' a death blow."[15]

For most pre-emancipation American history, however, the core property rights of slaveowners were accepted and enforced, built into economic behavior in ways that implied expectations of long-term viability for the institution. The one major exception was the abolition of slavery in the northern states after the Revolution, a break from a long history during which slavery not only existed in the North, but also was accepted without significant opposition. Abolition was extended westward in the 1780s by the exclusion of slavery north of the Ohio River in the North-west Ordinance, but even this ostensibly decisive measure did not have the finality to contemporaries that it was later assigned by history. The slavery issue was actively debated in the new states and territories during a crucial window in historical time, roughly from the 1780s to the 1820s. But these key state-level decisions proved effectively irreversible, at least through ordinary political channels, and the state policy issue virtually dropped from discussion on both sides of the Mason-Dixon. Even in slave states where slaveless farmers constituted a large majority of the free population, such as Kentucky and Missouri, slaveowners exercised decisive political power, and their rights were not seriously threatened.

Thus the compatibility between the political requirements of slavery and modern economic development was not seriously tested by American history, because the slave regime in the South was disrupted only by an extraordinary national military upheaval. Prior to that rupture, the country experienced its acceleration of economic growth in the nineteenth century "half slave and half free," under two dramatically different prop-

15. Robinson, "'Worser Than Jeff Davis,'" 14.

erty systems, each of which appeared to be stable both politically and economically within its own borders. Chapter 2 analyzes these two growth trajectories as a species of "cold war" competition between property-rights systems, endeavoring to explain not just why the two economies evolved differently but why their comparative performance has been subject to such varying perceptions and evaluations.

AN ECONOMIC PERSPECTIVE

The emphasis on property rights in these essays is in a sense standard practice among economists, though slavery has not received the same historical scrutiny from this perspective as other more conventional assets such as land. Some historical readers may find the terminology peculiar if not downright distasteful. My only defense is that the distaste is not in the mode of analysis but in the historical behavior under examination. When historians ask themselves just what was new about New World slavery, in comparison with other coercive regimes throughout history, they generally conclude that the difference was not in the degree of brutality, or in the intensity of the work, or even in the political domination of the masters. Instead, as Bernard Bailyn observes, the novel feature was that chattel slavery, a condition considered by Europeans to be appropriate only for the remote margins of civilization, was "here incorporated into a world of growing sophistication." Slaves produced crops for markets governed by complex systems of law and credit, products destined for consumers that were affluent and industries that were advanced by the standards of the day. Distasteful as it may seem to modern readers, slave economies functioned through elaborate legal and financial channels, as fully developed and in some ways more fully developed than their counterparts in the free-labor states. In a word, they were systems of property rights. Seen in this light, we can use relatively conventional economic tools to understand their historical consequences.[16]

But it should be acknowledged at the outset that an economic perspective is only a partial view of the subject. The culture and ideologies of slaves and slaveowners are not addressed in these chapters, and there is no

---

16. Bailyn, *Peopling of British North America*, 118.

claim here that these aspects of slavery are reducible to simple economic terms. Perhaps the most glaring omission is the absence of a discussion of the racial basis for American slavery. Even from the perspective of economic history, a full understanding would have to explain how it was that property rights in human beings came to be imposed on only one racially defined group. These issues have been extensively discussed by historians and economic historians, and it remains unclear whether the explanation lies mainly in the realm of economics or elsewhere. Whatever the outcome of that debate, the subject is not addressed here in any direct way.

One may argue, however, that *a* racial basis for slavery is implicit in the property-rights analysis advanced here. It is difficult to imagine that the property rights of slaveowners could have evolved in such a thorough-going, unconstrained manner, except by defining the enslaved as the "other" in extreme terms, not members of society or capable of becoming members in the course of time. Indeed, legal historians observe that the clarification and strengthening of property rights in slaves was intimately linked to intensified perceptions, ideologies, and rhetoric of racial inferiority. The Barbados slave code was also known as the "black code," and its preamble described Negro slaves as "an heathenish brutish and uncertaine and dangerous kind of people." South Carolina's supreme court stated in 1832: "By law, every negro is presumed to be a slave." Presumptions about race and presumptions about property were mutually reinforcing. A. Leon Higginbotham and Barbara K. Kopytoff summarize their review of the legal history of slavery in Virginia by writing: "The failure of the law to recognize any rights of the slave sprang from its view of the slave as property."[17]

In light of this historical duality, one may hope that an analysis of the implications of property rights in slaves will be useful for coming to grips with the racial as well as the economic basis for American slavery. A full account of this interplay, however, is beyond what these essays hope to accomplish.

---

17. For the early slave codes, see David Barry Gaspar, "'Rigid and Inclement.'" The South Carolina court is quoted in Finkelman, "Centrality of Slavery," 6. Higginbotham and Kopytoff, "Property First, Humanity Second," 534.

1

Slavery, Geography, and Commerce

In recent decades, economic historians have rediscovered both the centrality of African slavery for the eighteenth-century expansion of commerce
known as the Rise of the Atlantic Economy, and the importance of overseas markets for the industrial and technological breakthroughs known
as the Industrial Revolution. The number of Africans transported to the
Americas between 1700 and 1820 was five times larger than the number of free European migrants, and slave-based products dominated the
long-distance markets of that era. To invoke another phrase from an older
generation of economic historians, slavery was at the heart of the Commercial Revolution, which set the stage for the modern era of economic
growth. The process of coming to terms with these historical relationships has barely begun and will no doubt occupy us for some time into
the future.

This chapter assuredly does not undertake a full historical accounting,
but it addresses a question often neglected in the literature. What was it
about slavery that made it so vital to the emerging commercial economy?
The weight of the evidence suggests that the rise of African slavery in
the Americas was not primarily attributable to its advantages in production, but to the features identified in the introduction as property rights.
Propositions about the "relative productivity of slave and free labor" are
usually ambiguous for this simple reason: most of the time, slaves were
working at tasks and in locations that could not attract free workers on

commercially viable terms, so that we can never keep "other things equal" in making such comparisons. Labor relations and work performance varied widely, but this distinctive feature of slavery—the assignment of workers to tasks and geographic settings they would not voluntarily have chosen—was enduring and explains why slavery was crucial to the rise of the Atlantic economy.

WHAT HAS BECOME OF THE WILLIAMS THESIS?

Since its publication in 1944, Eric Williams's *Capitalism and Slavery* has stood as a benchmark or reference point around which discussions on the economics of the British slave trade and Caribbean slavery have revolved. In briefest summary, Williams maintained that the profitability of Britain's slave colonies caused or at least helped to establish conditions favorable to the Industrial Revolution of the late eighteenth century. As a corollary, Williams saw the movement to abolish the slave trade as driven by economic rather than humanitarian motives, reflecting the decline of the sugar economy and the emergence of new industrial economic interests. "Great mass movements," Williams concluded, "and the anti-slavery mass movement was one of the greatest of these, show a curious affinity with the rise and development of new interests and the necessity of the destruction of the old."[1] How has this provocative thesis fared in the wake of subsequent scholarship?

For a full generation, the Williams thesis was dismissed by Anglo-American writers as an exaggerated caricature, a reflection primarily of underlying hostility toward both the British and capitalism. But research of recent decades has gone far to confirm the essential accuracy of that portion of the argument putting slavery at the center of the commercial revolution that laid much of the foundation for the industrial revolution of the late eighteenth and early nineteenth centuries. African slavery was essential for Spanish, Portuguese, and Dutch trade in sugar, spices, and precious metals. In light of the high mortality rates of indigenous populations and the great difficulties experienced in recruiting European labor voluntarily, it was *only* African slavery that made it possible

1. Williams, *Capitalism and Slavery,* 211.

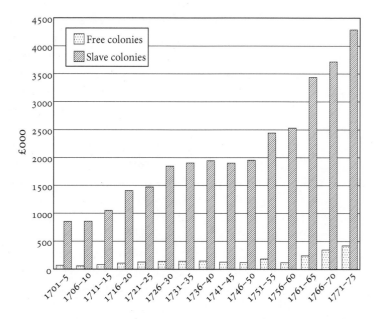

FIG. 1.1. British American exports to England (£000), 1701–75

Sources: U.S. Department of Commerce, Bureau of the Census, *Historical Statistics of the United States,* 1176–77; Schumpeter, *English Overseas Trade Statistics,* 18.

to exploit the commercial potential of colonial conquests. Barbara Solow points out that early transatlantic commerce was dominated by sugar, extending a pattern of slave-based tropical export agriculture that pre-dated Columbus, referred to by Philip Curtin as the "plantation complex." British colonization efforts were essentially failures from a commercial standpoint until Britain's entry into the slave-sugar network of the Caribbean in the seventeenth century.[2]

Prior to the nineteenth century, the "wealthiest and most dynamic regions of the Americas" were worked and populated primarily by slave labor. Figure 1.1 divides the exports to England from British North America into those from "slave" and those from "free" colonies, defining those terms retroactively according to the political choices made regarding

2. Solow, "Capitalism and Slavery"; Solow, "Slavery and Colonization"; Curtin, *Rise and Fall of the Plantation Complex.*

slavery after the American Revolution. It is obvious at a glance that slave-produced commodities were predominant and that their relative importance continued throughout the eighteenth century. If anything, figure 1.1 understates the matter, because it does not include the exports of Chesapeake tobacco to Scotland, which flourished from midcentury onward. At the time of the Revolution, total and per capita wealth levels of the slave colonies were far greater than those of their protofree counterparts.[3]

Long-distance trade was a leading sector for the British economy of the eighteenth century, growing more than twice as fast as national income. There is no economic magic in long distance per se: in the abstract, domestic demand may serve just as well as a stimulus for new industries. But in the mercantilist world of the eighteenth century, overseas markets lent themselves much more readily to rapid expansion through imperial linkage, and perhaps as much as 95 percent of the *growth* in the volume of British commodity exports went to imperial markets. In turn, the largest share of this growth was in trade with the Americas, as shown in table 1.1.[4] These British exports were exchanged for American goods, more than 80 percent of which were produced by African slave labor, as estimated by Joseph E. Inikori.[5] The result was, in the words of mercantilist Malachy Postlethwayt, writing in 1745, "a magnificent superstructure of American commerce and naval power on an African foundation."[6]

Taken together, the evidence suggests that there are more than a few grains of truth in the Williams thesis, long considered moribund. It was not that "slave trade profits" flowed through some fiendish channels into the dark satanic mills. But the burgeoning Atlantic trade of the eighteenth century derived its value from the products of slave labor and would have been much diminished in the absence of slavery.

3. Eltis, *Economic Growth*, 24. For wealth levels, see McCusker and Menard, *Economy of British America*, 61, based on the research of Richard Sheridan and Alice Hanson Jones. The wealth differentials are moderated by Peter Coclanis, "Wealth of British America," 259, but markedly extended by T. G. Burnard, "Prodigious Riches," 507, 517, 520. Additional supporting evidence on the primacy of slave colonies may be found in Galenson, "Settlement and Growth," 197–200; and Engerman and Sokoloff, "Paths of Growth," 263–75.

4. O'Brien and Engerman, "Exports and the Growth of the British Economy," 186.

5. Inikori, *Africans and the Industrial Revolution*, 197.

6. Quoted in Williams, *Capitalism and Slavery*, 52.

TABLE 1.1 Destination of English exports, 1663–1820

YEAR	EUROPE (%)	AMERICAS (%)	REST OF WORLD (%)
1663–69	90.5	8.0	1.5
1700–1	85.3	10.3	4.4
1750–51	77.0	15.6	7.4
1772–73	49.2	37.3	13.5
1797–98	30.1	57.4	12.5
1818–20	46.7	43.5	9.8

Source: O'Brien and Engerman, "Exports and the Growth of the British Economy," 186.

As sugar became an item of common consumption in Britain, the sugar trade provided a powerful stimulus for a diverse range of occupations and ancillary activities, especially in London.[7] The efficiency of ocean shipping improved markedly across the eighteenth century, not primarily through technological advances, but as a result of gains in economic organization and reductions in risk: a "revolution of scale" in the words of Jacob M. Price and Paul G. E. Clemens.[8] Two round-trips per year became the norm as opposed to one. The importance of overseas trade for institutional development in shipping, finance, and marketing can scarcely be exaggerated. According to Price, the most striking and distinctive peculiarity of British commercial organization in this period was the extension of long credits by warehousemen and wholesalers to exporters, contracts that depended on the scale of trade for their viability.[9]

Ultimately the Industrial Revolution was defined by the discontinuities in production technology that accelerated in the latter part of the eighteenth century. A full review of this venerable subject is well beyond the scope of these essays. But it is not inappropriate to observe that in recent decades both economists and historians have developed renewed appreciation for the role of expanding markets in encouraging innovations. In economics, the emerging body of thought known as "new growth theory"

7. Zahedieh, "London and the Colonial Consumer."

8. Price and Clemens, "A Revolution of Scale in Overseas Trade." On improved efficiency in shipping, see Gary Walton, "Sources of Productivity Change."

9. Price, *Capital and Credit in British Overseas Trade,* 117–18.

associates an expansion of market scale with an environment conducive to innovation.[10] Among economic historians, detailed accounts portray an endogenous transition from midcentury Smithian innovations in products and marketing to the more famous Schumpeterian inventions of the 1780s and 1790s, featuring many of the same industries and entrepreneurs. Even before 1800, the cotton textiles industry had reached a scale large enough to support specialized machine makers, whose ongoing innovations and marketing efforts served to spread the technologies of the Industrial Revolution around the globe in the nineteenth century.[11]

Can we say, therefore, that African slavery was the cause of the industrial revolution? One may argue with some justification that it is anachronistic to assign pivotal causal significance to one element (African slavery) in a larger structure, when that element was itself an endogenous outgrowth of centuries of seafaring, conquering, and planting by aggressive, expansionist Europeans.[12] We are in effect asking a hypothetical thought-question: whether the rise of the Atlantic trading economy could have occurred as it did if slavery had somehow been abolished centuries earlier. But why single out that necessary condition, as opposed to any number of others? Even if we do, if the objective is to explain the Anglo-American economic successes of the nineteenth century, its slave origins are clearly only a necessary and not a sufficient explanation. Whatever Britain had that Spain, Portugal, and Holland did not, access to slavery was not the differentiating factor. David Eltis has shown that Britain became the world's leading shipping nation by 1650, well before its involvement with the slave trade, a superiority that he attributes to superior credit facilities, lower cost of services, and the impact of the Navigation Acts in excluding Dutch competition. In turn, the productivity advantage in shipping

10. For one historical interpretation by the originator of "new growth theory," see Paul Romer, "Why, Indeed, in America?" The essential role of Atlantic trade and colonies in the rise of European national economies between 1500 and 1850 is demonstrated in a quantitative study by Daron Acemoglu, Simon Johnson, and James Robinson, "The Rise of Europe."

11. An analysis of the wool textile industry explicitly along these lines is presented by John Smail, *Merchants, Markets and Manufacture*. On the shifting locus of innovation in textiles, see Trevor Griffiths, Philip A. Hunt, and Patrick K. O'Brien, "Inventive Activity in the British Textile Industry"; and Christine Macleod, "Strategies for Innovation," 286–88.

12. See particularly Meinig, *Shaping of America*.

allowed the British to dominate the African slave trade by 1800, supplying not only its own colonies but those of Spain and other nations as well.[13] As the international economist Ronald Findlay argues, "slavery was an integral part of a complex intercontinental system of trade in goods and factors within which the Industrial Revolution, as we know it, emerged. Within this system of interdependence, it would make as much or as little sense to draw a causal arrow from slavery to British industrialization as the other way around . . ."[14]

How this history might have looked without slavery is not a question that arises naturally from known forks in the path of history. Such a question acquires its bite only from the perspectives of the nineteenth and twentieth centuries, when slavery had come to be an unthinkable barbarity and the institutional forms of England had come to be identified with something called capitalism. Slavery was somehow a central and integral part of the process, yet its effects became enduring and historically significant only in conjunction with other fundamental developments in the economic and technological world. Stanley Engerman points out that England's more dynamic development relative to France was not based on superior performance of the British sugar colonies compared to that of the French.[15] Evidently the critical ingredients lay elsewhere, or perhaps in the British imperial package taken as a whole.

It may be beyond us to say precisely the extent to which African slavery was indispensable to the rise of the modern economic world. What we can do is pose a question that is often not asked in this burgeoning literature: What was it about slavery that made it so central to commerce in the premodern world?

THE GAINS FROM SLAVERY: PRODUCTIVITY VERSUS PROPERTY RIGHTS

Central to the rise of African slavery in the Americas were the features identified in the introduction as property rights, specifically, the right of a slaveowner to employ the slave in a location and at an activity of

13. Eltis, *Rise of African Slavery in the Americas,* 37, 41, 114–36, 208.

14. Findlay, *"Triangular Trade" and the Atlantic Economy,* 28–29.

15. Engerman, "France, Britain and the Economic Growth of Colonial North America," 246.

the owner's choosing, ignoring any preferences on the part of the slave. Robin Blackburn has proposed a counterfactual history in which slavery had been banned very early, suggesting that the need to recruit free labor would have set development on a more positive social, political, and economic path. But other scholars reject this scenario as utterly anachronistic. David Eltis, who has devoted years to analyzing the evidence on transatlantic migration, concludes that more than 60 percent of all transatlantic migrants were African slaves prior to 1700, the share rising to 75 percent in the eighteenth century. It was not until the 1840s that voluntary European migration first exceeded the volume of the slave trade, and those Europeans who did come "generally stayed well away from the tropical zones." Similarly, Seymour Drescher writes that, for the kinds of enterprises in which slave labor predominated, "other forms of labor would have been available only at much higher prices."[16]

It is true that the early English plantations on Barbados and in the Chesapeake drew upon white indentured labor, an institutional form whose coercive features gave employers a degree of control that would hardly constitute free labor by modern standards. But indentured servitude was ultimately a contractual arrangement, voluntary in the sense that the servant could refuse the offer if the prospective employment were sufficiently grim. David Galenson's econometric estimates show that servants bound for the West Indies received shorter terms (by as much as eight to nine months) than those going to the mainland, indicating that the mainland was strongly preferred. Those who did go to Barbados hastened to leave as soon as their terms were completed. Only when indentured servitude was replaced by slavery did British Caribbean population and exports grow significantly; from that point forward, the white population ceased to expand and in fact declined (fig. 1.2). Small wonder: death rates exceeded birthrates by a considerable margin, so that the population grew only through a continuing influx of African slaves (fig. 1.3). Mortality was generally better on the mainland. But in South Carolina, efforts to attract or retain Irish labor were generally unsuccess-

16. Blackburn's counterfactual is presented in *Making of New World Slavery*, 357–62. Eltis's migration estimates are presented in *Rise of African Slavery in the Americas*, 8–11; and in "Free and Coerced Migrations," 34, 60–74. The Eltis quotes are from *Economic Growth*, 14, 165. The Drescher quote is from "White Atlantic?" 39.

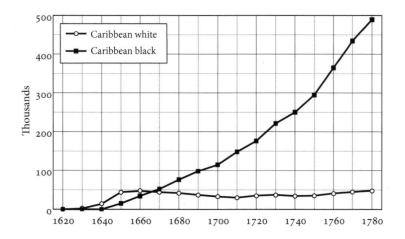

FIG. 1.2. Population of British Caribbean, 1620–1780
Source: McCusker and Menard, *Economy of British America,* 153–54.

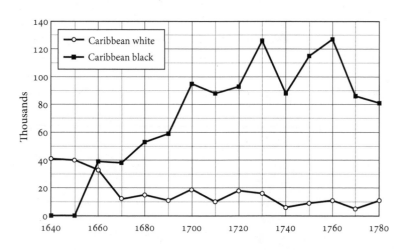

FIG. 1.3. Net migration to British West Indies, 1630–1780
Source: Galenson, "Settlement and Growth of the Colonies," 178, 180.

ful because of negative publicity and persistent rumors that terms of servitude would be extended involuntarily. Competition with other colonies forced a reduction in the length of contracts, while statutes imposed caps on terms and required that servants receive clothing and provisions when their terms were completed. The major advantages attributed to African slave labor were that terms of service were unlimited and that labor supply was unresponsive to adverse rumors.[17]

In addition to locational preferences, work in the sugarcane fields—the destination of perhaps two-thirds of African slaves—was associated with death rates that were substantially higher than those resulting from work with other crops. According to Philip D. Morgan, sugar entailed "literally a killing work regime" for reasons of both the hostile disease environment and episodic stress. It did not take long for word to spread: white labor in Barbados "soon learned of [sugar's] rigors and avoided it at all costs."[18] In light of these conditions, it is difficult to see how the Atlantic sugar trade could have flourished as it did in the absence of slavery or something similar to slavery. As mercantilist Sir James Steuart asked in 1767: "Could the sugar islands be cultivated to any advantage by hired labor?"[19]

Perhaps these points are obvious, almost part of the definition of slavery as "involuntary servitude." Yet for some reason historians often seem to feel obliged to explain the rise, spread, and persistence of slavery in terms of advantages in productivity, commonly associated with the intensity of the work pace. Thus Barbara Solow writes that slave labor was "elastically

17. Galenson, *White Servitude in Colonial America*, 110. The sources for South Carolina are Peter H. Wood, *Black Majority*, 40–43; and Russell R. Menard, "Africanization of the Lowcountry Labor Force," 86–88. Karen Kupperman reports that "a general impression of unhealthiness" hung over the southern colonies: "Fear of Hot Climates," 236. Philip Coelho and Robert McGuire argue that a difference between Africans and Europeans in biological susceptibility to disease has been neglected as a factor in explaining the spread of African slavery in the New World, raising the possibility that the racial differential in death rates was increased by the shift to an African labor force. This hypothesis does not contradict the view that recruiting a voluntary labor force to these locations would have been extremely difficult; indeed, it reinforces the conclusion that the sugar trade could not have expanded as it did in the absence of slavery. See "African and European Bound Labor in the New World."

18. Morgan, "The Poor: Slaves in Early America," 302, 313; Dunn, "'Dreadful Idlers' in the Cane Fields."

19. Quoted in Drescher, *Mighty Experiment*, 17.

supplied and especially productive in crops of widespread importance," while Eltis asserts (citing nineteenth-century evidence) that "the productivity advantage lay with the coerced rather than the free labor regions of the Atlantic." At times Eltis seems virtually to equate work intensity with productivity, as when he describes American slavery as involving "exploitation more intense than had ever existed in the world," and then proceeds to elaborate in the next sentence: "It is inconceivable that any societies in history—at least before 1800—could have matched the output per slave of seventeenth-century Barbados or the nineteenth-century Southern United States." In a recent volume, Eltis, Frank D. Lewis, and Kenneth L. Sokoloff declare: "Generally, family-based farming anywhere in the Americas and the urban and port activities that grew up to service them could not generate the productivity performance of slave societies."[20]

This insistence on a productivity advantage for slave labor is doubly puzzling, both because it is unnecessary and largely peripheral for understanding the centrality of slavery to the rise of Atlantic commerce and because there is virtually no evidence in support of these claims. The editors just quoted assert that "the empirical evidence [for a productivity advantage and productivity growth under slavery] is overwhelming," but their only citation is to Robert Fogel's *Without Consent or Contract,* which deals with the late antebellum U.S. cotton economy. The antebellum evidence receives detailed attention in chapter 3. For the moment, it suffices to say that even if Fogel's findings for the cotton crop year 1859–60 are accepted at face value, this would not constitute a strong basis for assertions pertaining to the Caribbean sugar economy in earlier centuries. For the seventeenth century, Eltis himself laments the absence of plantation records "to even verify the existence of productivity improvements, much less pinpoint their source."[21]

Opportunities for direct comparison between free- and slave-labor performance are rare indeed, because free and slave labor rarely coexisted, doing the same tasks in the same place at the same time—for reasons

20. Solow, "Transatlantic Slave Trade," 12; Eltis, *Rise of African Slavery in the Americas,* 7, 18; Eltis, Lewis, and Sokoloff, *Slavery and the Development of the Americas,* 23.

21. Eltis, Lewis, and Sokoloff, *Slavery and the Development of the Americas,* 24; Eltis, *Rise of African Slavery in the Americas,* 214, 220.

that should be obvious in light of the foregoing discussion. In the atypical cases where slaves and free laborers did coexist—such as the colonial iron industry or agriculture in the northern colonies—labor performance standards were generally found to be indistinguishable. A preference for slaves was attributed to "the needs of industrial stability," a clear reference to the property rights of an owner of labor.[22] During the relatively brief transition period on Barbados, the physical productivity of slave and indentured-servant labor was reported to be equal.[23] A similar transition took place in the Chesapeake at the end of the century, of which Russell R. Menard writes: "Chesapeake planters did not abandon indentured servitude because they preferred slaves; rather, a decline in the traditional labor supply forced planters to recruit workers from new sources, principally but not exclusively from Africa . . . Chesapeake planters did not abandon indentured servitude; it abandoned them."[24]

On the basis of her detailed study of plantation accounts, farm diaries, and probate records, however, Lorena Walsh does conclude that "the switch from predominantly servant to predominantly slave labor did raise productivity on the majority of plantations," a finding seized upon by Blackburn as support for the intensification hypothesis.[25] It would be ironic indeed if the best support for the work-effort hypothesis came from tobacco, a crop that persisted as a family-farm bastion for centuries. On closer examination, however, Walsh's evidence is far from conclusive. Walsh does refer to a "more stringent work routine," but she also describes an extension of work hours (including night work), an increase in the number of workdays, and participation of women in field work, all of which constitute an expansion of labor inputs rather than productivity.

22. Lewis, *Coal, Iron, and Slaves*, 230. For another example, see John E. Stealey, "Slavery and the Western Virginia Salt Industry": "Contemporary salt manufacturers believed that slave labor was superior for their industrial needs because of cheapness, supply, and stability . . . In the Salines, there was never enough free labor available for employment in all phases of the salt industry. The real alternative was between no or insufficient labor or slave labor, and the manufacturers did not hesitate to make the necessary choice" (129, 130–31).

23. Beckles and Downes, "The Economics of Transition," 238.

24. Menard, "From Servants to Slaves," 355, 389.

25. Walsh, "Slave Life, Slave Society, and Tobacco Production," 174–83; Blackburn, *Making of New World Slavery*, 315–25.

Even if we set aside this conceptual distinction, Walsh's figures provide no evidence of any *sustained* increase in tobacco output per laborer under slavery (175, table 7.1). Productivity may have peaked during the transition, but it subsequently declined in nearly every one of the plantation clusters displayed. As Walsh acknowledges, the data for corn and wheat show no productivity differential of any kind. Even for tobacco, the variation among plantation clusters in both productivity levels and trends is so wide that one would be hard pressed to support any strong conclusion about slavery as a work system from this information.

This is not to argue that productivity growth under slavery was not possible or that it never occurred. Because slaveowners as a rule were acquisitive and responsive to economic incentives, it would be surprising if they ignored opportunities to increase profits by raising production per slave. In his study of West Indian slavery, J. R. Ward compares figures from the years 1739–48 for average sugar production per estate slave with those from 1820 to 1834, suggesting an increase of perhaps one-half of 1 percent per year in Barbados and Jamaica, though not in the Leeward Islands. Nearly all of the productivity growth, however, began in the period 1799–1819, during which the African slave trade was abolished and slave prices rose. Ward reports that the productivity increase in Jamaica "was achieved without any increase in hard driving." So much for the equivalence of productivity and work intensity—Jamaican productivity figures reported by B. W. Higman show no productivity growth even for the late pre-emancipation period.[26]

The most careful study of agricultural productivity on the British mainland is for South Carolina, a colony whose plantation crops (rice and indigo) were more readily adaptable to gang labor methods than was tobacco. Yet Peter C. Mancall, Joshua L. Rosenbloom, and Thomas Weiss find that "long-run [1720–1800] productivity improvements were modest at best, and may have been negative." Cruder indicators such as exports per worker do show rapid growth for shorter periods (particularly 1750–1770), but these are attributed by the authors to fluctuations in demand conditions and in mercantilist policies (such as the bounties on

26. Ward, *British West Indian Slavery*, 91, 94; Higman, *Slave Population and Economy in Jamaica*, 213 and *Montpelier, Jamaica*, 44.

indigo introduced in the 1740s), and they did not survive the Revolution. When account is taken of production for domestic consumption as well as for export, the estimates show essentially no productivity growth during the colonial era, with perhaps a slight positive drift between 1770 and 1800—driven by growth in food exports to other states, not by exports to foreign destinations.[27]

Does this issue really matter? The distinction between property rights and productivity has implications for understanding the relationship between slavery and modern economic development. If we picture slavery as a superior (if harsh) form of production, we are led to ask why and how market-oriented societies in England and America managed an extraordinary feat of self-denial, by cutting off the life support for and then abolishing this institution at steep private cost to the nation. But if instead we understand the gains as deriving from something like arbitrage, a set of property rights that made possible a range of valuable market transactions that otherwise would have been long delayed, then we will see slavery more as Eric Williams did, as an institution well adapted to the age of mercantilism and commercial revolution.[28]

27. Mancall, Rosenbloom, and Weiss, "Agricultural Labor Productivity in the Lower South," esp. 390, 393, 419–21.

28. After the manuscript for this chapter had been submitted, an article appeared in which the authors attempt to estimate the rate of productivity growth under Caribbean slavery indirectly, using information on the relative change in the prices of slaves and sugar. (David Eltis, Frank D. Lewis, and David Richardson, "Slave Prices, the African Slave Trade, and Productivity in the Caribbean, 1674–1807," *Economic History Review* 58 [2005]: 673–700.) The authors conclude that "total factor productivity in slave agriculture increased markedly" over the period 1674–1790 (696). This result, however, depends entirely on the assumption that slave-maintenance expenditures increased at the same rate as the value of output (measure A), a conjecture for which no evidence is offered. Under the more plausible specification that slave-maintenance expenditures were independent of output value (measure B), the implied productivity increase is only 10.7 percent over the entire period, which is to say virtually zero (682). In addition, the narrowing spread between slave prices and sugar prices can also be attributed to declining interest rates, and to greater efficiency in the transportation of sugar. The first of these is acknowledged in the article (681, 685); the second is unjustifiably dismissed (685). Thus, contrary to the authors' assertions, the logical inference to be drawn from the exercise is that the "gang system of slave labor" could not have generated major productivity gains in Caribbean agriculture.

AFRICAN SLAVERY AND THE
BRITISH AMERICAN MAINLAND

Americans have found it particularly difficult to come to terms with our "slave origins," perhaps because the national history of the United States makes it easy to forget that the thirteen mainland colonies were only a part of the larger trading network of the British Empire, and the northern states all abolished slavery within two decades of the American Revolution. But in the colonial era, slavery was legal in all parts of British America, and it was economically significant even in many areas that later became free states. Slave labor was used successfully in such high-fertility areas as the Narragansett Bay in southern New England, the Connecticut and Hudson river valleys, Long Island, and the grain-producing regions of eastern Pennsylvania and northern New Jersey. Between 1725 and 1750, according to Ira Berlin: "Slaves became the single most important source of labor in the North's most fertile areas and its busiest ports. . . Slaves [in these areas] were no longer an adjunct to an agricultural economy based on family labor or white servitude but were the largest element in the rural labor force."[29]

For the mainland, as for the islands, historians often seem to feel obliged to interpret the geographic distribution of slaves in terms of slavery as a form of work organization. When I ask beginning students to explain why 90 percent of mainland slaves were found in the southern colonies (those that later became slave states) as of 1770, their answers generally cluster around two themes: ideology or the aptness of the fit between certain crops and purported features of slave labor—slave crops are thought to be more labor-intensive or perhaps more effort-intensive than free-labor crops. The first hypothesis can be firmly ruled out. Ideological opposition to slavery was politically insignificant in all parts of British North America prior to the American Revolution as demonstrated by David B. Davis in *The Problem of Slavery in Western Culture.* Slaves were in demand and the laws of slavery were enforced throughout the empire. The major complaint of the northern colonies was that they could not buy

---

29. Berlin, *Many Thousands Gone,* 179, 181. See also Christopher Hanes, "Distribution of Slave Labor in Anglo-America," 307. The "slave origins" quote is from Jack P. Greene, *Pursuits of Happiness,* 2.

as many slaves as they wanted, at prices they could afford to pay, which is another way of saying that they were outbid in the market for scarce African slaves.

Why then did the southern colonies have the advantage in the bidding for slaves? Certainly not because of any inherent congruence between southern crops and slave labor. Roughly two-thirds of mainland slaves worked on tobacco, which dominated mainland exports throughout the colonial era, but tobacco growing has virtually none of the attributes commonly associated with a need for coerced labor. Yes, tobacco required much labor over the course of the year, but the tasks were diverse and care-intensive, calling upon (according to Gloria Main) "the kind of knowledge acquired only through long experience and diligent attention to detail." The quality of the product made all the difference in its value, and a single slip at any one of the key steps (harvest, curing, and packing) could effectively destroy a year's labor. In other words, tobacco would seem to be ideally suited for small-scale family farming, and so it has been through most of its history. Some plantation managers learned how to operate somewhat larger operations profitably in the eighteenth-century Chesapeake, but their success turned largely on expanding production of corn and wheat rather than on advances in slave-based production of tobacco per se. Although rice and indigo in the Lower South may have required slave labor for their economic viability (on the Caribbean pattern), for the tobacco regions it is more appropriate to say that slavery *displaced* a comparable volume of free farm labor that would otherwise have found its place in this sector.[30]

Broadly speaking, mainland agricultural slavery located where farmland was most valuable, so that the *value* of labor's product was high enough to cover the price of a slave. In this formulation, the value of farmland must be understood to reflect more than the intrinsic fertility of the

---

30. Main, *Tobacco Colony,* 31–38; Carr and Menard, "Land, Labor, and Economies of Scale," 407–18; Walsh, "Plantation Management," 393–406. On South Carolina, one early observer wrote: "The low lands of Carolina, which are unquestionably the richest grounds in the country, must have long remained a wilderness, had not Africans, whose natural constitutions were suited to the climate and work, been employed in cultivating this useful article of food and commerce." Quoted in Menard, "Slavery, Economic Growth, and Revolutionary Ideology," 271.

soil—on which count much of the southern Piedmont would not rank high—but also the climatic requirements for valuable crops such as tobacco and later cotton. A third important factor was access to markets, which in the colonial era largely meant proximity to the coast or to inland waterways. Where these elements were present, slavery was quite compatible with production of corn, oats, wheat, and other crops commonly associated with small family farms. When Chesapeake planters shifted into grains, work routines and skill requirements changed, but slaves were fully occupied, and slavery persisted. In the northern colonies, slave labor was employed successfully on the most fertile and best-located soils. But over most of these regions during the colonial era, the value of farm labor productivity was simply not high enough to support slaves.

Yet slavery was central to the economies of the northern as well as the southern colonies, not mainly through the direct presence of slave labor, but indirectly, through sales to markets that originated with slave-based production. The British Empire constituted a complex interdependent mechanism, a general equilibrium economic system protected against outsiders by military superiority.[31] As imperial insiders, the northern colonies were beneficiaries of this regime. Table 1.2 shows the predominant role of slave-based commerce for New England and the Middle Atlantic. As late as 1768–1772, the British West Indies were the largest single market for northern-colony commodity exports, accounting for more than half the overall total and dominating sales of such items as wood products, fish, and meat. Trade with the West Indies was the major stimulus for early development of the infrastructure of port cities in these colonies, including harbors, warehousing, insurance, and financial services. Manufacturing activity was also facilitated, particularly rum distilleries and sugar refineries. John J. McCusker and Russell R. Menard write: "By the 1770s West Indians were importing a variety of manufactured goods from the continental colonies, from cheap earthenware to furniture and vehicles. The implications of this trade for the economic development of the colonists on the continent were immense."[32]

31. An analysis of empire relationships as a general equilibrium system is presented in Findlay, "*Triangular Trade*" and the Atlantic Economy, building upon earlier work by William A. Darity Jr., "Eighteenth-Century Atlantic Slave Trade."

32. McCusker and Menard, *Economy of British America*, 288–94.

TABLE 1.2 Average annual value and destination of commodity exports from New England and Middle Atlantic colonies, 1768–72 (pounds sterling)

COMMODITY	GREAT BRITAIN	IRELAND	SOUTHERN EUROPE	WEST INDIES	AFRICA	TOTAL
Fish	206		57,195	94,754		152,155
Livestock, beef, pork	2,516		1,660	105,810		109,986
Wood products	8,618	4,982	4,405	76,614		94,619
Whale products	40,443		804	20,416	440	62,103
Grains, grain products	15,570	9,709	179,278	194,725		399,282
Rum	471	44	1,497		16,754	18,766
Other	77,520	38,256	2,523	9,359	1,077	128,735
Total	145,344	52,991	247,362	501,678	18,271	965,646

Source: McCusker and Menard, *Economy of British America*, 108, 199, using data from Shepherd and Walton, *Shipping, the Maritime Trade, and the Economic Development of Colonial North America*.

Another perspective on these trends is shown in figure 1.4, which presents figures on the value of imports from England for the same groupings of colonies used in figure 1.1. The contrast between the two figures is striking. Though the imports of the slave colonies were initially larger, the growth of imports into the free colonies was much faster, so that on the eve of the Revolution the two were nearly equal. How was it possible for free-colony imports to be so much larger than commodity exports from those same colonies? One part of the answer is in the rise of "invisible" trade, payments to noncommodity services such as shipping and finance, probably the single largest credit item in New England's balance of payments. Because they neglect invisibles, the figures in table 1.2 understate the involvement of the northeastern colonies in slave-based commerce. But a second part of the answer cuts the other way: the proliferation of new trade triangles across the eighteenth century, so that the volume of coastal commerce was nearly equal to overseas trade by the 1770s. The juxtaposition of figures 1.1 and 1.4 underscores the changing character of economic relations within the empire. As of 1775, the slave-based economy was still central to the interdependent imperial trade network. But British producers, looking for markets for manufactured goods, in-

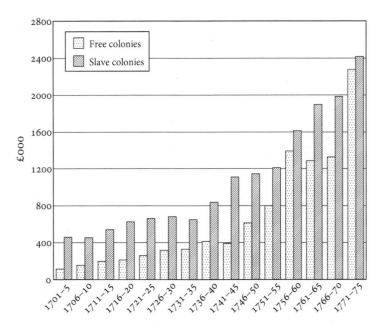

FIG. 1.4. British American imports from England (£000), 1701–75
Sources: U.S. Bureau of the Census, *Historical Statistics of the United States*, 1176–77;
Schumpeter, *English Overseas Trade Statistics*, 17.

creasingly turned their attention to areas where slaves were few. Benjamin
Franklin observed the emerging pattern as early as 1760: "The trade to
our Northern Colonies, is not only greater, but yearly increasing with the
number of people: and even in a greater proportion, as the people increase in wealth and the ability of spending as well as in numbers."[33]

In the eighteenth century, the difference in regional demand growth
was mainly driven by the relative growth of the free populations in the
two groups of colonies (fig. 1.5). Long before the slave trade was closed,
and despite the uniquely favorable demographic experience of slaves
on mainland North America, white population growth in what were to

33. Franklin, "Interest of Great Britain Considered," in *Papers of Benjamin Franklin*, ed.
Labaree, 9:87. On New England's invisible exports and coastal trade, see Margaret Ellen
Newell, *From Dependency to Independence*, 74–75. On the rise of the North American mar-
ket for British exports, see S. D. Smith, "British Exports to Colonial North America," 45–63.

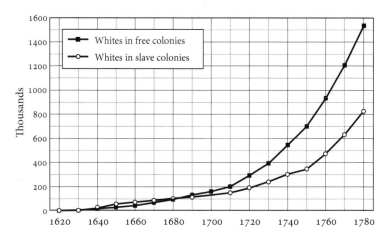

FIG. 1.5. White population in British America, 1620–1780
Source: McCusker and Menard, *Economy of British America*, 103, 113, 137, 153, 154, 203.

become the free areas was vigorously outpacing the growth in the slave colonies. At work was a different growth dynamic, in which the active encouragement of free migration was central. Bernard Bailyn has written:

> The slave trade was only the extreme expression of the deliberate engineering of overseas migration. William Penn's famous efforts at promoting emigration and settlement . . . were relatively passive: in effect Penn ran an advertising campaign sufficient to mobilize elements of a readily available population. But in time truly dynamic entrepreneurs of migration appeared, and the flows of emigration to North America were propelled forward by them . . . And the recruiters could succeed because the maturing American economy, while superficially providing less of an open opportunity than it had earlier, was basically more expansive, more elaborate, more attractive than it had been before, and its magnetism persisted, at times grew.[34]

As Franklin observed, the expansion of the free population was augmented by growth in its "ability of spending," as the effort to attract settlers led the northeastern colonies to support development activities such as town-founding, subsidies for enterprise, and elaboration of the distribu-

34. Bailyn, *Peopling of British North America*, 86.

tional infrastructure, including roads, ports, markets, shops, and newspapers. These activities were not absent in the southern colonies, but even before the Revolution, they were far more extensive in the north.[35]

Bailyn's account is compelling, but the reference to the slave trade as an "extreme expression" of the same impulse obscures the fundamental contrast, indeed the incompatibility, between the two processes. One misgiving about the slave trade was the idea that slaves displaced free migrants, and that areas dominated by slave labor reached a "tipping point" beyond which free migration was positively discouraged. In the lowcountry of South Carolina, for example, the white population quickly declined with the advent of slavery after 1700. Richard Dunn notes that the economic successes of the British in the Caribbean were not widely publicized; he counts no more than eight or ten promotional tracts in a century, numbers exceeded almost every year in colonies like New Jersey and Pennsylvania.[36]

In depicting the "peopling of British North America" as an outward extension of long-developing patterns of domestic mobility in Europe, Bailyn neglects the earlier and larger forced migration of Africans to the New World and the importance of their slave labor to commercial development and trade. It is easy to do so when viewing the world from the northerly perspectives of the mid-eighteenth century onward. Slavery had not declined, and the relative eclipse of slave-based commerce did not derive from new problems of work discipline or inefficiency. But at that time, an image of an entirely different world of commercial expansion without slavery began to seem believable.

THE RISE OF ANTISLAVERY AND
THE PROBLEM OF COLLECTIVE MEMORY

The rapid rise of British antislavery between 1783 and 1807 has stood as a challenge to generations of economic historians, withstanding all efforts

35. See particularly Margaret Ellen Newell, *From Dependency to Independence*, 57–70, 91–108; David Hancock, "Revolution in the Trade," 127–36; T. H. Breen, *Marketplace of Revolution*, 104–47.

36. Menard, "Slavery, Economic Growth, and Revolutionary Ideology," 260, 271; Dunn, *Sugar and Slaves*, 23.

to interpret political change as a rational response to economic incentives. To Eric Williams it was all quite clear: "The commercial capitalism of the eighteenth century developed the wealth of Europe by means of slavery and monopoly. But in so doing it helped to create the industrial capitalism of the nineteenth century, which turned around and destroyed the power of commercial capitalism, slavery, and all its works." The problem with this part of the Williams thesis is not merely that it is all but impossible to identify an important interest group whose economic interests were served by abolition. Even if the thesis is understood in broader ideological or even metaphorical terms, how could such an epochal transformation have been compressed into such a brief space in time, "instantaneous in historical terms," in David Eltis's phrase? Slavery was a large and integral part of the modern economic world, and then with relative suddenness slavery seemed to become entirely inessential to economic progress—even a positive hindrance—everywhere except where slaves in large numbers were actually held. Drescher cites the example of Arthur Young as typical of many who revised their views on the practical implications of abolition and then "implied that they had known for an age what they had discovered only yesterday."[37]

If we accept the premise that the conversion to antislavery was "historically instantaneous," we will indeed have an impossible task linking that change in sentiment to deep historical phenomena. Blackburn and Drescher have pointed toward one way to restore some of these links, by noting that popular antislavery had much older and more evolutionary roots in the decline of serfdom throughout western Europe. The spread of local opposition to bound labor long predated the major philosophical critiques of slavery, and took the form of demands for exclusion of slavery from a given town or territory. The tradition that slaves became free the moment they set foot (or breathed the air) of particular districts predated the African slave trade. With the rise of the nation-state, the "free air" principle became an aspect of emergent national identity in England, France, and the Netherlands. Rarely the object of general legislation, the principle had a shadowy standing, somewhere between a folk precept and

---

37. Williams, *Capitalism and Slavery,* 210; Eltis, *Economic Growth,* 4; Drescher, *Capitalism and Antislavery,* 86.

a common-law doctrine. Yet it was often accepted by the courts, as in the 1762 case *Shanley v. Harvey:* "As soon as a man sets foot on English ground he is free: a negro may maintain an action against his master for ill usage, and may have a *Habeas Corpus* if restrained of his liberty." When Chief Justice Mansfield ruled ten years later in the *Somerset* case that a slave could not be forcibly removed from England, a celebrated decision later seen as a watershed for the abolitionist movement, he drew upon traditions that were centuries old.[38]

What changed at the end of the eighteenth century, therefore, was not so much the discovery of a fundamentally new concept in human relations but the emergence of a political movement *universalizing* what until then had been largely a local and territorial impulse. This insight helps to explain the speed of change. What is notable for our purposes is the dualistic or two-sided character of the free-air principle. On the one hand, it reflected views about what was proper in human relationships, a sense of the wrongness of enslavement. But on the other hand, it had an exclusivist side, a statement of pride in national identity, coupled with a determination to prevent established relationships from being disrupted by the intrusion of slave-like arrangements. In this latter guise, the free-air principle was associated with what might be called high-wage thinking in eighteenth-century Britain, the belief that higher rewards for labor would stimulate effort levels and raise productivity—Adam Smith being a prominent proponent.[39] Whereas the older notions were broadly European, the tendency to universalize them to the world at large was distinctively British.

But does this formulation imply that the antislavery conversion was a purely ideological experience, unconnected with real developments in the economy? Williams maintained that the crusade against slavery arose only after the Caribbean sugar islands entered into historic economic decline, so that "any impartial observer, if such existed, could have seen

38. Blackburn, *Overthrow of Colonial Slavery,* 36–37 and "Background to European Colonial Slavery," 87–89. Drescher, *Capitalism and Antislavery,* 16–22. Peabody, "There Are No Slaves in France," 3–5, 12–14. *Shanley v. Harvey* is quoted in Higginbotham, *In the Matter of Color,* 329.

39. Coats, "Changing Attitudes to Labour," 35–42.

that their time was up." The effort to confirm or refute this "decline" thesis has proven highly frustrating to cliometricians, impartial or not. In his pathbreaking 1977 book *Econocide,* Seymour Drescher reversed the Williams formulation diametrically, arguing that there were no signs of decline in the colonial sugar economy until abolition cut off the supply of slave labor to the islands. Almost to the end of the trade in 1807, slaves were in strong demand, sugar production and exports were rising, and the West Indian colonies still employed half the nation's long-distance shipping, while sugar duties supplied an eighth of Exchequer revenues. In rebuttal, Selwyn Carrington maintains that the Caribbean planters never fully recovered from the shock of the American Revolution, when the islands were cut off from essential supplies of lumber and food, and that in the decades preceding abolition the British sugar industry showed many signs of being "an economy in distress."[40]

This debate is difficult to resolve, both because the subject matter is as much subjective as objective and because the years in question were so dominated by warfare that we have no normal times within which to assess the prospects of the sugar economy. The most telling evidence of decline is not based on failure in production but on indications that the real price of sugar had been in steep decline for ten years prior to abolition, a phenomenon sometimes referred to as overproduction. Figures collected by David Beck Ryden show that deflated Jamaican Muscovado sugar prices peaked in 1797 (after a surge in the 1790s triggered by the slave revolution in St. Domingue) and then fell to record lows between 1802 and 1807. The decline in slave values during this period scarcely suggests an economic class brimming with optimism. Many contemporaries felt that planters were lukewarm in their opposition to abolition, and parliamentarians supporting the measure noted its value as a method of reducing excess sugar production. The crisis of 1807 was short-term, dominated by political-strategic as much as by economic considerations, not by deep fundamentals of capitalism or laissez-faire economics. But

---

40. Williams, *Capitalism and Slavery,* 211; Drescher, *Econocide,* 16–36, 65–79; Carrington, *Sugar Industry and the Abolition of the Slave Trade,* 91–115, 221–45; Ward, "British West Indies in the Age of Abolition," 427.

clearly the West Indian slave-sugar interest was losing political clout well before the ultimate vote to abolish the slave trade.[41]

It would be a major mistake to interpret the abolition of the slave trade as the result of a narrow economic calculus of costs and benefits. The planters themselves opposed the move on balance, and it is undeniable that British slave-based sugar growing would have had a rosier future (on newer islands such as Trinidad as well as the older producing centers) if the African slave trade had continued. Yet it is equally undeniable that perceptions of the economic costs and benefits were changing, not least because of the explosive growth in British industrial production, the bulk of which was exported to the nonslave markets of the world. On this count as well, visible economic trends offered a kind of liberation for longer-standing (but submerged) views on adverse *economic* aspects of slavery. Davis suggests that "as early as the mid-eighteenth century, slave societies were acquiring the image of social and cultural wastelands blighted by an obsessive pursuit of private profit." Overseas slavery was seen as degenerate and corrupting, affecting whites as well as blacks. What protected slavery from outside attacks prior to the 1790s was not a positive belief in the institution, but a sense of its remoteness and unreformability, perhaps a kind of relativism-cum-racism by which practices unacceptable at home (or within a national-ethnic group) might regrettably have to be tolerated abroad. Above all, slavery, like warfare, was rationalized as essential to the wealth and power of the empire. Opinions changed rapidly, not because people were buying into a whole new belief system about incentives and work effort, but because they no longer felt that slavery was essential to national welfare. As Ward summarizes the case: "The abolitionist cause prevailed in 1807 because moral arguments were reinforced by changing circumstances, which made it seem that Britain could now safely dispense with the slave trade . . . British abolition was not merely cynical and self-interested, but neither did its authors believe that they were making a significant economic sacrifice."[42]

41. David Beck Ryden, "Does Decline Make Sense?" esp. 365, 372. On American shipping competition, see Francois Crouzet, "Crisis of the British Imperial Economy," 303–15.

42. Davis, *Slavery and Human Progress,* 80; Drescher, *Capitalism and Antislavery,* 20; Ward, "British West Indies in the Age of Abolition," 427–28.

Were the British abolitionists correct in this belief? Rather than approach this as an objective question with a single correct answer, it would be more appropriate to conceptualize the process as an exercise in collective learning. At the turn of the nineteenth century, the Age of Adam Smith, in which growth was dominated by exploitation of gains from expanding markets, was giving way to the Age of Schumpeter, as entrepreneurship moved into the search for innovation in technology and improvements in processes of production. This change in the mode of economic progress was associated with a broad northward shift in the geographic center of gravity of the Atlantic economy, under way well before the American Revolution. As British talents moved into high-technology production of manufactured goods, the sugar islands came to seem remote and irrelevant to the important things in economic life, as indeed they were. Despite the continuing importance of slave-based commerce as of 1807, it would be difficult to claim that abolition and emancipation inflicted significant damage on the British economy.

Abolitionism and antislavery sentiment emerged early in this whole process, before the British capitalist self-image coalesced into the ideological package of free trade, free labor, and free markets. In effect the British went through a collective learning process, coevolutionary with decisive breaks in their political and economic history. With the American Revolution, they learned that they could lose a major colony without disrupting economic progress. With abolition, they learned that they could give up the slave trade without damage to the economy, indeed without significantly increasing the price of sugar. When emancipation did cause a rise in the price of sugar in the 1840s, they found a remedy in free trade—a convulsive episode that humiliated the abolitionists and split the previously existing coalition.[43] Thus it would be quite wrong to interpret the entire abolitionist record as governed by a commitment to laissez-faire ideology. Yet it is not always inappropriate to reason backward from later consequences to prior causes, since if any of these lessons had been seriously wrong—as they might have been fifty to one hundred years earlier—antislavery momentum might well have been markedly slowed.

43. Drescher, *Mighty Experiment,* 158–76.

In this sense we can say that Eric Williams had his finger on the right correlation, though the "curious affinity" between abolition and industrialization may have been more curiously circuitous than he imagined.

SLAVERY AND FREEDOM IN THE UNITED STATES

The antislavery political revolution had its counterpart in the newly independent republic as well. The ideological currents underlying the swing against slavery were broadly similar in the two cases. But in North America, the practical realities of slavery were far more pressing and immediate, hearkening back to the setting within which the free-air principle emerged in European towns and districts. Efforts by urban artisans to exclude slave labor from particular trades began in the seventeenth century and were often successful. In New York City, for example, blacks were barred from carting or portering by legislation enacted in 1677. Opposition grew across the eighteenth century in Boston, New York, Philadelphia, and other northern cities. "Significantly," writes Winthrop D. Jordan, "it is often impossible to ascertain from the language of these protests whether they aimed only at slave labor or at free Negro labor as well." To the extent that the motive was to restrict competition in the labor market—a feature of which the language of the petitions generally left no doubt—it was logical for the petitioners to neglect or obscure this distinction. But from the 1760s onward, artisan petitions took the form of objection to all forms of bound labor within a city's jurisdiction. These colonial-era campaigns did not threaten slavery as an institution. But they molded a constituency upon which abolitionists could build after the Revolution.[44]

Although the causes of the American Revolution will be debated to eternity, it is safe to say that the decision for independence was not motivated by a desire to free slaves. The British charge of hypocrisy still stings, most tellingly in Samuel Johnson's jibe: "How is it that we hear the loudest yelps for freedom from the drivers of negroes?" Yet the Revolution and political independence precipitated movements that led to the abolition of slavery in all the northern states, shortly after the turn of the nineteenth

44. Hodges, *New York City Cartmen*, 25; Jordan, *White over Black*, 128–29; Nash, *Urban Crucible*, 109–10, 320–21, 343–45; Zilversmit, *First Emancipation*, 46–47, 227.

century. Even in Massachusetts, slavery was "firmly entrenched" in 1776, and it was "only in the context of the Revolution that the antislavery movement gained support outside a fringe group of Quakers and other agitators." Most historians attribute the shift in prevailing opinion to the glaring inconsistency between revolutionary rhetoric and the reality of slavery—an "excruciatingly conspicuous" incongruity that free blacks did not hesitate to publicize.[45]

It is perfectly true that slaveholders in the southern states had relatively little difficulty overcoming this problem of cognitive dissonance, so that abolition only occurred in states where slaves were relatively few. But this fact does not mean that the northern abolitions were of merely marginal historical significance. Slaveowners in states like New York and New Jersey fought long and hard to maintain their property rights in slaves, so that the policy shift was the outcome of an intense political struggle. The success of these campaigns was only possible because politically independent American states had the right to make such decisions. The abolition of slavery in the British Empire came only in 1833, more than a full generation later. How different would the contours of North American history look if slavery had continued to expand north as well as south of the Mason-Dixon line?[46]

The early abolition of slavery in northern states generated what Joanne Melish calls "virtual amnesia about local slavery" in the Northeast. In time this collective memory loss was extended to the entire northern half of the country, through the effects of what was arguably an even more significant byproduct of the American Revolution, the exclusion of slavery north of the Ohio River by Article VI of the Northwest Ordinance of 1787. Most northerners and probably most historians presume that this provision merely ratified the realities of economic geography, that slavery never took root in the northwest territories because it was not well suited

45. The quotes on Massachusetts are from Joanne Pope Melish, *Disowning Slavery,* 50, 56. The phrase "excruciatingly conspicuous" is from Gordon Wood, *Radicalism of the American Revolution,* 186. On the use of the Declaration of Independence as "an abolitionist tract" by free blacks, see Benjamin Quarles, "Antebellum Free Blacks," 229–42; and Thomas J. Davis, "Emancipation Rhetoric," 248–63.

46. The most careful review of alternative scenarios relating the Revolution to abolition is David B. Davis, "American Slavery and the American Revolution," 262–80.

to midwestern farming conditions. But such perceptions are powerfully colored by subsequent historical events, from abolition in the Northeast to the Civil War itself. In reality, if the decision had been left to the first generation of settlers in these areas, they would have voted for slavery. Between 1787 and 1807 residents of the Ohio territory inundated Congress with petitions urging repeal of Article VI. Although these petitions were ignored, no steps were taken to free any slaves under the provisions of Article VI, and indeed new slaves were brought into the territory during this period. After Ohio statehood in 1803, the majority position in the Indiana Territory was clearly proslavery, led by Territorial Governor William H. Harrison, himself a wealthy slaveholder from Virginia. Only when it became clear that Congress would not repeal Article VI did the Indiana territorial legislature resort to a system of indentured servitude that amounted to a de facto slave code. Numerous auctions and advertisements testify to the reality of slavery in the region. Only the threat of congressional veto induced Indiana to enter the Union as a free state in 1816.[47]

Who was behind this opposition to the extension of slavery, and what were their reasons? The origins of Article VI are shrouded in mystery. It was drafted in haste and approved by the Continental Congress without debate, receiving support from southern as well as northern delegates. It has sometimes been portrayed as a proslavery measure, because it effectively foreclosed earlier attempts to prohibit slavery in all the western territories, and it contained a fugitive-slave clause calling for the return of runaways (a provision missing from the Articles of Confederation). Some accounts credit the lobbying activities of Manasseh Cutler, representative of the New England investors who formed the Ohio Land Company. The company planned to buy five million acres of land in Ohio, and it is possible that Cutler (who presented some proposed amendments to the committee the week before the ordinance was adopted) insisted on the slavery prohibition as part of the deal. But the evidence for this reading is inconclusive, and Congress did not follow up with enforcement measures that would have confirmed a serious intent to effect revolutionary social

47. Melish, *Disowning Slavery*, 220; Finkelman, "Evading the Ordinance," 35–40; Rosenberg and McClurg, *Politics of Pro-Slavery Sentiment in Indiana;* Thornbrough, *Negro in Indiana before 1900*, 6–8, 26–28.

change on the western frontier. Only in hindsight did the Northwest Ordinance take on its character as landmark antislavery legislation. What
we can say is that opposition to the extension of slavery stiffened with the
passage of time, as the north-south contrast in regional settlement patterns became visible.[48]

During the Constitutional Convention, it was generally assumed that
settlement and population growth would be most rapid in the southern
states, where cash crops promised quick financial returns. During a debate on representation and taxation in July 1787, Rufus King declared:
"He must be shortsighted indeed who does not foresee that whenever
the Southern States shall be more numerous than the Northern, they can
& will hold a language that will awe them [the Northern states] into justice." Gouverneur Morris added: "It has been said that North Carolina,
South Carolina, and Georgia only will in a little time have a majority of
the people of America." Hence the willingness of the South to accept a
compromise on representation in the new federal Congress, believing that
"this government . . . will be very shortly in our favor."[49]

Early in the nineteenth century, however, observers began to notice
that just the opposite was occurring, as migration into the free territories
dramatically exceeded expectations. It did not take long for the difference
to be associated with the choice of labor systems. Even wealthy southerners invested in lands north of the Ohio River, believing that these were a
better financial prospect than lands to the south. Thus, over time the slavery debate in the Northwest took on a different economic shape. Proslavery forces advanced the old economic case, arguing that rapid settlement
and commercial development in remote frontier areas could only take
place through the use of slave labor. This proposition was advanced not
just by self-interested slaveowners, but also by landowners who believed
that the growth of land values would be diminished by effectively prohibiting the entry of "valuable immigrants" from the South. This argument

48. Finkelman, "Slavery and the Northwest Ordinance," 345–53; Onuf, *Statehood and
Union,* 110–31; Zeitz, "The Missouri Compromise Reconsidered," 471–85.

49. Quoted in Lynd, *Class Conflict, Slavery, and the U.S. Constitution,* 173–74. The "in our
favor" statement is by Wilson Nicholas, a southern Federalist. See also Finkelman, "Slavery
and the Constitutional Convention," 199.

was forcefully pressed in the pitched debate that took place in Illinois in the mid-1820s. Slavery advocates portrayed their adversaries as throwing away money for the sake of ideology: "Look at those trains of wagons with their splendid teams, their carriages and their gangs of negroes. They are going to fill up Missouri, and make it rich, while our State will stand still or dwindle, because you won't let them keep their slaves here."[50]

In each of the territories in turn, this view was overtaken by an influx of settlers from the Northeast. To be sure, there were elements of regional culture clash in the debate. But the economics of land values were not far below the surface. Changing perceptions of these relationships may have been decisive in Illinois, where the 1824 debate over a proposed new state constitution was in effect a referendum on slavery. Rev. Thomas Lippincott, corresponding secretary for the "Madison Association to oppose the introduction of Slavery in Illinois," pointed out that both population and land values increased more rapidly in Pennsylvania than in Virginia, concluding that "the existence of slavery in one, and its non-existence in the other state, has caused the discrepancy."[51]

Did these evolving perceptions of slavery's economic effects have any impact on the geography of slavery? Kentucky illustrates one case in which an early beachhead effectively perpetuated slavery, even in a state that might have been considered not naturally suited for slave-based agriculture. Because Virginia retained Kentucky when it ceded other western land claims, the area was unaffected by the Northwest Ordinance, and slaveowners were able to enter freely. But the 1790 census identified only 1,855 slaveholders in Kentucky, in a total population of 61,000, with an average holding of just 6.7 slaves. Because Kentucky farmlands were the objects of a jumble of conflicting ownership claims in the 1790s—making it a "paradise for lawyers" as much as for farmers—many settlers feared that slavery threatened prospects for broad-based land acquisition by facilitating the aggrandizement of large holdings.[52]

50. The report of slaveowner investment in Ohio is from a letter from George Nicholas to James Madison, 2 May 1792, quoted in Harrison, *Kentucky's Road to Statehood*, 125. The Illinois quote is from Suzanne Cooper Guasco, "Deadly Influence," 21.

51. Quoted in Guasco, "Deadly Influence," 23.

52. U.S. Bureau of the Census, *Negro Population in the United States*, 56 (table 5), 57 (table 6).

Despite this opposition, Kentucky slaveowners were far better represented and better focused on their goals than were their opponents at the 1792 convention. Ninety percent of the delegates owned slaves, two-thirds of them holding five or more. Slavery was the only issue contentious enough to require a roll-call vote, on which the antislavery amendment was defeated by 26 to 16. Opposition to slavery played a role in the subsequent campaign for a new constitutional convention. But when that campaign finally succeeded in 1799, the convention actually strengthened the legal status of slavery, denying the legislature authority to prohibit importation of slaves into the state. In later decades, even though most public discussion proceeded from the premise that slavery was economically harmful, abolition became politically unthinkable, both as a violation of the rights of owners and because of the perceived need to control the black race.[53]

In contrast to Kentucky, the rich river-bottom lands of southern Illinois were considered ideally suited for slavery by many settlers. With corn yields as high as 100 to 120 bushels per acre, these lands were said to be "the most fertile of any in the Union," attracting many early migrants from the South. There were perhaps 1,000 slaves in Illinois at the time of statehood in 1818, enough to prompt an English settler to write that it was "as much a slave-state as any south of the Ohio River." Illinois entered the Union as a free state for the same reason as Indiana: it was well understood that Congress, concerned about maintaining balance between free and slave states, would not approve a state constitution any other way. Although the true sentiments at the constitutional convention favored slavery, the leadership managed to persuade the majority that after statehood, the new legislature would then be free to reenact the old territorial black codes. Thus, as in Kentucky (but in the reverse direction), approval of statehood did not end the slavery debate in Illinois. The call for a new constitutional convention originated with proslavery forces, but in August 1824 the proposal was defeated by a vote of 6,640–4,952. Although slavery was not legally abolished in Illinois until 1845, the anticonvention vote of 1824 ended the discussion and settled the issue as a practical matter.[54]

53. McDougle, *Slavery in Kentucky*; Harrison, *Kentucky's Road to Statehood*, 2–11, 103–19; Aron, *How the West Was Lost*, 89–95; Tallant, *Evil Necessity*, 7–9, 107.

54. Quoted in Guasco, "Deadly Influence," 16. See also James Simeone, *Democracy and Slavery in Frontier Illinois*; and Harris, *History of Negro Servitude in Illinois*.

Just how different the economic and political history might have been if the vote had gone differently in 1824, it is impossible to say. What we can say is that slavery was a live prospect on the Northwest frontier. It was not excluded by geographic imperatives or the demands of particular crops—slavery could thrive outside the cotton and tobacco regions, as it did in Missouri's Little Dixie and in the wheat-growing areas of antebellum Virginia—but by a sea change in prevailing opinion (at least among northerners) with economic as well as broader ideological elements. If the proslavery forces had prevailed long enough to establish an economic as well as a political beachhead, slavery might have shown as much persistence in Illinois as in Kentucky. But something about slavery gave these political decisions a formative, either-or character: where slavery was maintained, abolition became undiscussible; where slavery was abolished or excluded, it dropped from collective memory.

As an illustration of the change in consciousness, consider the language of the Indiana Supreme Court in the 1821 case of *Mary Clark, a Woman of Color*. The dispute grew out of an attempt (one of many) by a slaveholder to evade the law by claiming that a servant had voluntarily signed a long-term labor contract. The court declared:

> It may be laid down as a general rule, that neither the common law nor the Statutes in force in this State recognize the coercion of a specific performance of contracts . . . Such a performance, if enforced by the law, would produce a state of servitude as degrading and demoralizing in its consequences, as a state of absolute slavery; and if enforced under a government like ours, which acknowledges a personal equality, it would be productive of a state of feeling more discordant and irritating than slavery itself.[55]

Thus, while debate over slavery raged in Illinois, and only five years after reluctant acceptance of the decision against slavery in Indiana, a court defined what sounded like national identity in terms of the absence of slavery. It is no exaggeration to say that as of that historical moment, the United States was not one country but two.

---

55. Quoted in Steinfeld, *Invention of Free Labor*, 144. Steinfeld considers the Clark decision a landmark in the rise of a distinctively American conception of free labor.

For the era prior to the American Revolution, it makes little sense to invoke slavery as the cause of regional economic differentiation. Slavery existed in all parts of British North America, and the geographical distribution of slaves may be interpreted in terms of supply and demand: the demand side featuring the location of major export crops, but also the climatic preferences of immigrants, specialized demands for household servants, and doubtless other factors; the supply side dominated by the operation of the African slave trade, competition from elsewhere in the Americas, and demography. But with the abolition campaigns in the northern states, and the exclusion of slavery from the Northwest Territory, slavery emerged as a decisive *institutional* distinction between two contiguous groups of states. We thus have a rare opportunity to observe the record of economic development under two distinct institutional regimes, a nineteenth-century version of cold-war competition between rival economic systems.

2

Property and Progress in Antebellum America

For some years debates about the economic character of the antebellum South have fallen into a peculiarly constraining groove. "Was the slave South capitalist?" has been the question, taken to be the same as asking whether typical slaveholders were calculating, acquisitive, and in pursuit of material goals through markets. According to the terms of this discourse, the ascendancy of the view that American slaveowners were "rational capitalists" and slavery a "flexible, highly developed form of capitalism" thereby implies that the course of the *economy* of the slave South was essentially similar to that of the capitalist North.[1] But this is a non sequitur. Property owners in the two regions may have been more- or less-equally calculating, acquisitive, and in pursuit of material goals through markets—to the extent that we can ever hope to calibrate these sorts of subjective psychological traits for any society—but it would not follow that the two regional economies should closely resemble each other, because slavery and free labor were very different sets of institutional arrangements. That human relationships would be different under slavery is hardly surprising. That relationships between economic progress and the land were also very different is perhaps less obvious. Demonstrating that difference is the central purpose of this chapter.

1. Fogel, *Without Consent or Contract,* 64. An explicit statement on the similarity of the two capitalist regions is made by Edward Pessen, "How Different from Each Other?" See also Laurence Shore, *Southern Capitalists.*

I propose that we view the antebellum era as a kind of cold war on the North American continent, in which two different economic systems set out to generate wealth through territorial expansion. At the starting line in 1790, the two economies were nearly equal in population, area, and levels of wealth. Broadly speaking, they shared a similar cultural and legal heritage. So the economic competition boiled down to the institutional difference between them. We know who won the hot war that ended this historical era, but military prowess in itself is surely not an adequate or acceptable measure of the performance of an economy. Who won the antebellum economic cold war and how we should read the scoreboard of regional performance have long been in dispute. A central reason for this intellectual stalemate is that appropriate measures of economic success depended on property rights, and each region had reason to declare itself the victor on its own terms.

FREE LABOR AS AN INSTITUTIONAL INNOVATION

We begin with a defense of the premise that after about 1790 the establishment of free labor in the North and slavery in the South represented a true institutional difference between the regions. Ever since the publication of David Brion Davis's *Problem of Slavery in Western Culture* in 1966, it has been understood that moral opposition to slavery emerged as an important historical force only in the second half of the eighteenth century, in North America as in Britain. Prior to the American Revolution, slavery was legally enforced and socially accepted in all of the British American colonies, North as well as South. But when prevailing opinion shifted, as it did in the northern states, the change was decisive and fundamentally irreversible. The Revolution itself was an important ideological crystallization. As early as 1777, the new Vermont state constitution provided that "no male person, born in this country, or brought from over sea, ought to be holden by law, to serve any person, as a servant, slave or apprentice, after he arrives to the age of twenty-one years, nor a female, in like manner, after she arrives to the age of eighteen years, unless they are bound by their own consent, after they arrive at such age, or bound by law, for the payment of debts, damages, fines, costs, or the like . . ." Pennsylvania's gradual emancipation law followed in March 1780. All of the New England states had abolished slavery within a year of the war's end. The last northern holdouts, New York and New Jersey—the two with the highest shares of slaves in their populations, at 7.6 percent in 1790—fell into line in 1799 and 1804, respectively.[2]

The North-South divide in the response to this new thinking was unmistakable. The first draft of the Northwest Ordinance, written in 1784, would have banned slavery from *all* of the western territories as of 1800. It failed in repeated votes, and the logjam was only broken in 1787 when the prohibition was restricted to the area north of the Ohio River. At the Constitutional Convention, the same regional split was evident on all issues pertaining directly or even indirectly to slavery. As Madison recorded: "It now seemed to be pretty well understood that the real difference of interest lay, not between the large and small but between the northern and southern states. The institution of slavery and its consequences formed the line of discrimination."[3]

To be sure, it is always easier to declare a change irreversible after the fact, with the aid of hindsight. The Continental Congress may have legislated an end to slavery north of the Ohio in 1787, but no specific steps to free the slaves in the Northwest Territory were actually undertaken during this period. As reviewed in chapter 1, proslavery majorities existed early in the settlement phases of Ohio, Indiana, and Illinois. The issue seemed in flux as late as 1824, during the debate over a new constitutional convention in Illinois. If slavery remained debatable in the Old Northwest long after the turn of the century, how then can we say that an irreversible division in institutional regimes was established as of the 1790s?

In answer to this challenge, note that there was a clear geographic pattern to this northern political economy of slavery: slavery was favored in the most remote territories, because property rights in labor offered the possibility of more rapid settlement and increases in land values than would be attained by the slow westward progress of voluntary migration. But as free settlers began to enter in large numbers, the political major-

2. Bruns, ed., *Am I Not a Man and a Brother.* See p. 432 for the text of the Vermont Constitution. The standard account of the northern abolitions is Arthur Zilversmit, *First Emancipation.*

3. Madison, *Notes of Debates,* 295.

ity invariably swung around to an antislavery position. For squatters and others aspiring to gain legal title to land of their own, the prospect of competition from wealthy slaveowners was seen as a threat, and for good reason. The accelerated westward migration of free settlers confirmed and solidified the antislavery majority. Thus the abolition of slavery in the Northeast, coupled with the opening of the Northwest Territory to settlement by free aspiring landowners, generated a political majority that effectively ratified the earlier decision for free labor.

This political logic was augmented and codified by court decisions, which eradicated not just slavery but indentured servitude as well, and severely weakened other forms of voluntary service such as apprentice-ship. According to legal historian Robert J. Steinfeld's *Invention of Free Labor,* a tipping point came when slaveowners tried to enroll their newly freed former slaves in long-term contracts as servants. In Pennsylvania, the increase in post-slavery indentures was amplified by an influx of French-speaking planters from St. Domingue, accompanied by their former slaves who (so they claimed) had agreed to terms of indenture averaging thirteen years in length.[4] These thinly disguised subterfuges tended to discredit all forms of long-term labor contracts in the northern states. The landmark Indiana decision quoted in the previous chapter (*Mary Clark, a Woman of Color*) arose in precisely such a case.

A fundamental post-Revolutionary shift was the abandonment of the doctrine of "specific performance," which compelled work for a particular employer. Although the timing is uncertain, because the issue was never the object of decisive legislation, it appears the decriminalization of labor contracts was largely complete by the 1820s. Perhaps the most direct evidence of change is found in the records of the Philadelphia municipal courts, which were heavily involved in "absconding from service" cases into the 1790s, typically punished either by incarceration or specific enforcement, i.e., return to the master. Such cases became rare after 1800, as law enforcement turned to crimes against the general public, such as drunkenness or vagrancy, and masters revised their business

---

4. Steinfeld, *Invention of Free Labor,* 138–43; Salinger, *"To Serve Long and Faithfully,"* 146–47.

strategies from apprehension to replacement. It is possible that most of those accused of absconding were in fact indentured servants, but David Montgomery reports that the court records are frequently vague about the precise status of the workers involved. Enforcement of indentures became more difficult in any case, because of the "popular antipathy toward bondage for white people." The nature of the problem is suggested by the experience of Ludwig Gall, a German immigrant to Pennsylvania who in 1819 had advanced passage money to a number of fellow Germans, intending to employ them as servants until the debts were repaid: "They had scarcely come ashore when they were greeted as countrymen by people who told them that contracts signed in Europe were not binding here; that even though they had indentured themselves, they were as free as birds here . . ." Though Gall saw clearly that these "riff-raff" were trying illegally "to tempt my people away," his effort to enforce the contracts by throwing the passengers into debtors prison only added to his expenses and was soon abandoned.[5]

Over time, northern legal precepts evolved toward a radical form of free-labor doctrine in which employees were entitled not just to quit without notice, but to receive compensation in *quantum meruit* for the work time they had already put in. The English common law was clear not only that an indefinite contract was an annual one, but that such a contract was "entire" (i.e., an indivisible whole). Initially, American courts upheld this doctrine and denied partial compensation for early quitters, for example in the influential Massachusetts decision of 1824, *Stark v. Parker*. Peter Karsten traces the gradual spread of an alternative American doctrine. In the 1834 case of *Britton v. Turner*, the New Hampshire Supreme Court decided in favor of a plaintiff who had agreed to work as a farmhand but had quit after nine months and sued for $100. A jury awarded him $95. The court's opinion held that a farmer who contracted for services "for a certain period" did so "with full knowledge that he must, from the nature of the case, be accepting part performance from day to day." A rule requiring payment for service actually received, the court ruled, would leave "no temptation to the employer to drive the laborer from his

5. Montgomery, *Citizen Worker*, 27, 33–34; Trautman, "Pennsylvania through a German's Eyes," 40.

service near the close of his term, by ill treatment, in order to escape from payment." Two years later, Vermont's supreme court adopted a hybrid variant, while other states held firmly to the English rule. But during the 1850s, *Britton v. Turner* was accepted by courts in Indiana, Connecticut, Michigan, and Iowa, and by Massachusetts in 1864. The evolution was almost exclusively a northern phenomenon: the only slave state to adopt the newer rule prior to the Civil War was Missouri.[6]

In this, however, the law was only catching up to norms of behavior on the ground. In the northern states, American labor markets were transformed in the decades following the Revolution, and formerly authoritarian employers had to cope with high levels of turnover and mobility among their workers. Winifred Rothenberg reports that, by 1800, Massachusetts farmers followed the practice of paying wages to workers who quit in breach of contract, well before the courts gave legal status to the *quantum meruit* principle. She suggests that this extreme form of free labor may have been "America's genuinely 'peculiar institution,'" possibly a New England innovation. But Sharon Salinger describes a marked rise in turnover at the artisan shops of Philadelphia beginning in the 1780s, where journeymen came and went so frequently the shops resembled "immigrant way stations."[7]

One should not infer that the norms and institutions of American free labor were firmly in place in the early nineteenth century. It would perhaps be more accurate to say that as of the 1820s, the right to quit was on an upward trajectory, to be legally consolidated only by the Civil War, the Thirteenth Amendment to the Constitution, and the Anti-Peonage Act of 1867. The "employment at will" doctrine—the presumption that an indefinite hire is terminable at any point by either party—was clearly articulated only in 1877 by treatise writer Horace Gray Wood.[8]

6. Karsten, "'Bottomed on Justice'" and *Heart versus Head,* 157–89. James D. Schmidt concludes: "By the time of the Civil War, labor contract law had diverged along sectional paths," noting that most southern cases dealt with overseers, upholding the employer's right of dismissal (*Free to Work,* 44–52).

7. Rothenberg, *From Market-Places to a Market Economy,* 181; Salinger, "Artisans, Journeymen, and the Transformation of Labor," 72 and *"To Serve Long and Faithfully,"* 155.

8. Wood, *Treatise on the Law of Master and Servant;* Morriss, "Exploding Myths," 683–89.

Indeed in the antebellum era, many judges upheld the *Stark* ruling's entirety principle for farm labor, arguing that it would be unreasonably burdensome for workers to quit before the harvest was complete. There were many attempts by farmers to gain continuity by offering what economists would call incentive-compatible contracts, for example through performance contingencies or assured harvest premia. Despite these efforts, farm labor was notoriously unstable and unreliable, seasonal contracts frequently broken because of dissatisfaction or better offers elsewhere, even at the risk of forfeiting wages. As one Michigan agriculturalist observed in 1850: "Custom has almost destroyed the obligation of contracts between the employed and the employer. The first thinks he has a right to leave whenever he pleases, and the last expects he will go when he likes."[9]

The same "norm of high mobility" (in Steinfeld's phrase) pervaded the first wave of American industrialization in the free states. In the factories and workshops that sprang up after 1815, workforce turnover was legendary. The giant Lowell-Waltham mills were the most famous of the enterprises that built an expectation of rapid turnover into their management systems and even into the physical plant itself, in the form of dormitories to accommodate young, unmarried women for periods of one to three years. Job tenures were even shorter in mills employing the family based Slater or Rhode Island system. Some firms did try to implement twelve-month contracts to reduce turnover, but generally without success; the companies often found themselves rehiring workers who had quit before the contracted full year. After 1830, most contracts were for shorter periods, in practice not effectively different from the minimal enforcement provided by two- or four-week pay periods.[10]

In my view it is not helpful to portray these developments as an unfolding of abstract principles of market capitalism, as many historians do. Labor norms and institutions evolved very differently in the United States than in England or continental Europe, and to this day, short job tenures and "at will" employment contracts distinguish the United States from

9. Quoted in Schob, *Hired Hands and Plowboys,* 221. On the difficulty of recruiting and retaining farm labor in the free states, see ibid., 85–91, 221–27; Schmidt, *Free to Work,* 38–44; and Fleisig, "Slavery, the Supply of Agricultural Labor, and Industrialization," 573–74.

10. Prude, *Coming of Industrial Order,* 150–54; Ware, *Early New England Cotton Manufacture,* 266; Zonderman, *Aspirations and Anxieties,* 155.

most other economically developed countries of the world. The at-will doctrine has often been seen as a class-based device for thwarting labor unions, and it was no doubt often invoked for this purpose.[11] But it also represented a deeply felt conviction about the meaning of freedom in America, as well as a practical reality to which employers had to adapt. As Charlotte Erickson has pointed out, there were mines, ranches, and rail-road- and road-construction enterprises in nineteenth-century America, often in remote locations and desperately short of labor, who would have been only too happy to import indentured servants, by then known as contract labor. But they did not have that option. With the single exception of Chinese labor used in the far west prior to 1882, contract labor was not successful in the United States. However we might characterize or evaluate this free-labor system, we can safely say that it constituted an institutional regime distinct from that of the antebellum South.[12]

Thus, free labor entered deeply into the culture and behavioral norms of the northern states, even while the southern states were solidifying their attachment to slavery. The southern side of the story is a familiar chestnut of American history: a brief flirtation with the post-Revolutionary ideology of freedom was soundly squelched by the rise of cotton as a cash crop after 1790—not by the invention of the cotton gin (as the old chestnut goes), but by the rise of British cotton demand during the first Industrial Revolution, matched with the South's unique natural status as a cotton-growing region. Together, these developments put slavery on a firm economic and political footing, and set the stage for the experiment in comparative institutional history that followed.

SLAVERY AND REGIONAL PROGRESS

Having characterized the institutional divergence, what indicators of regional economic performance should we now examine? Economists often assume that the only legitimate measure of aggregate economic perfor-

---

11. On the use of free-labor law against unions, see Brody, "Free Labor, Law, and American Trade Unionism."

12. Erickson, "Why Did Contract Labor Not Work?" The Chinese labor contracts were not enforced by American law but by Chinese companies who maintained control over return tickets. See Cloud and Galenson, "Chinese Immigration and Contract Labor."

mance is the total value of output, something like real gross national or gross domestic product, the sum of the value of all goods and services produced in an economy, adjusted for changes in the price level. The next step is to divide by population, because otherwise we could not very well compare levels of GDP for economies that are very different in size. Per capita output is certainly an informative magnitude, and historical economists have devoted many years of expert labor to constructing national and regional GDP series covering long stretches of history. But GDP is only one among many relevant criteria. Per capita GDP is to some degree unhistorical in that it represents the modern egalitarian perspective, by which each member of the economy deserves to be represented in a measure of that economy's performance. This certainly was not the dominant view in the slave South. A parallel question may be raised about including the incomes of future immigrants in the performance measures for the free states. Further, GDP is an annual-flow concept, subject to short-term fluctuations and not necessarily a good reflection of the success of the members of an economy in accumulating stores of present and future value to expand their range of choices at each point in time, to provide for security in old age, and to pass on to their descendants. For these purposes, wealth and wealthlike cumulative measures are generally better. Since our purpose here is not really to declare a single overall winner in this cold war on the continent but to understand the implications of institutional arrangements for comparative economic evolution, it might be better at this point not to commit to a single all-purpose performance measure but to keep our minds open to consequences that mattered to historical players in their own times.

Suppose then, that we put ourselves in the shoes of that first generation of founding fathers in the 1780s and 1790s and ask how the course of future progress might have looked to them. Each group of regional leaders was setting out to create value from the wide-open spaces to the west. At the starting line, the two regions were remarkably similar in size and economic status. Table 2.1 shows that the North and the South were within 150,000 persons of each other as of 1774, and the gap was a mere 7,000 as of 1790. Estimates of regional wealth developed by Alice Hanson Jones reveal a similar comparability in 1774. As seen in table 2.1, total wealth in the South was about 20 percent greater than in the North, nearly 40 per-

TABLE 2.1 Regional wealth in 1774

	13 COLONIES	NORTH	SOUTH
Population (thousands)	2,354	1,248	1,105
Wealth (thousand pounds)	109,570	49,052	60,518
Nonhuman wealth (thousand pounds)	88,106	47,918	40,188
Real-estate value (thousand pounds)	60,221	32,458	27,763
Wealth per capita (pounds sterling)	46.5	39.3	54.7
Nonhuman wealth per capita	37.4	38.4	36.4
Nonhuman wealth per free capita	48.4	41.1	61.6

Source: Jones, *Wealth of a Nation to Be*, 37, 51, 54, 58, 90.

cent greater on a per capita basis. But this difference is wholly attributable to the value of slaves and servants. Measured by nonhuman wealth per capita (real estate, livestock, and equipment and inventories of producers' and consumers' goods), the two regions were within 5 percent of each other: 38.4 pounds sterling for the North versus 36.4 pounds sterling in the South.

On the basis of table 2.1, one would have difficulty making a case that slavery had retarded economic progress in the South in the colonial era. True, more than one-third of southern wealth consisted of the value of slaves. But by the measure closest to a modern standard, the level of non-human wealth relative to total population, the South was nearly equal to the North. By an index better suited to the times, nonhuman wealth per member of the free population, the South was ahead by 40 percent. Thus, even if we omit the value of slaves as a component of wealth (as contemporaries surely did not), table 2.1 implies that slave labor made possible an accumulation of wealth for the free population of the South that put them considerably ahead of their northern counterparts.

Given this starting point, how did regional growth compare in the nineteenth century? One possible criterion is population. Table 2.2 shows that although both populations grew over time, the northern total began to move ahead after 1800. The population gap was 20 percent in 1820 and widened to 45 percent by 1840—even before the mass Irish potato famine—and was more than 80 percent by 1860. The North nearly doubled the South in population growth over a sixty-year period, primarily because

TABLE 2.2 Population, 1774–1860 (in thousands)

REGION	1774	1790	1800	1820	1840	1850	1860
South	1,105	1,961	2,622	4,419	6,951	8,983	11,133
Non-South	1,248	1,968	2,687	5,219	10,112	14,210	20,310
Northeast	1,248	1,968	2,636	4,360	6,761	8,627	10,594
North-central			51	859	3,351	5,404	9,097
West						179	619

Sources: Jones, *Wealth of a Nation to Be*, 37; U.S. Bureau of the Census, *Historical Statistics of the United States*, 22.

of the overwhelming northerly propensities of immigrants to the country. As measured by the preferences of free people voting with their feet, perhaps the North was winning the race.

No one would claim that population growth per se is an adequate measure of economic performance. But it might be a reasonable proxy from the perspective of the landowning classes. Population growth is a proximate determinant of increases in land values, and table 2.3 shows that by 1850, the North more than doubled the South in total value of farmland and buildings. Part of this difference reflected the North's greater political success in extending its authority into the north-central and western regions, adding vast stretches of low-value territory to the regional totals. But this difference in geographic expansion was by no means incidental, reflecting as it did the vigorous recruitment of and responsiveness by free migrants. Even if we restrict the comparison to a value-per-farm-acre basis, however, the northern margin of success was still greater, tripling that of the South as of 1850. In 1860, after the most prosperous cotton-boom decade in history (and a considerably more mixed period for the northern economy), the regional ratios still stood at nearly two-to-one in favor of the North in total farm value, and well over two-to-one in farm value per farm acre.

An increase in land value is an appropriate measure of wealth accumulation for a society as well as for private owners, albeit only one component of the total. To be sure, land values reflect natural attributes such

TABLE 2.3 Farmland values, 1774–1860

REGION	FARMLAND AND BUILDINGS (million dollars)			VALUE PER FARM ACRE (dollars)	
	1774	1850	1860	1850	1860
South	115	1,056	2,323	6.18	10.32
Non-South	135	2,216	4,322	18.02	23.75
Northeast	135	1,455	2,122	26.45	34.79
North-central		752	2,130	11.94	19.72
West		9	70	1.80	5.38

Source: Jones, *Wealth of a Nation to Be*, 37, 90 (1774 pounds sterling converted to dollars at $4.15; see p. 10); U.S. Bureau of the Census, *Historical Statistics of the United States*, 460–62.

as soil fertility and location, as well as human inputs. Alice Hanson Jones found that 1774 real-estate values per wealthholder were substantially greater in the South than in New England or the Middle Colonies, a difference she attributed to inherent superiority in climate and proximity to water, as well as to drainage, clearing, and building construction, largely by slave labor.[13] Whatever the relative contributions of nature and investment as of 1774, the *gains* in real-estate values across subsequent decades reflected human actions. This attribution is clearest in the distinction between unimproved and improved acreage, a type of capital formation based on labor devoted to land-clearing, with both a private cost and a private return. By this criterion the North was far ahead of the South: nearly 60 percent of land on northern farms was improved in 1860, versus one-third of the land on southern farms.

But even where gains in land values resulted from improvements in transportation and the advance of settlement—Henry George's "unearned increment" to the individual landowner—they still may be viewed as a form of wealth accumulation from the perspective of society. To the extent that rising land values were associated with population growth, of

13. Jones, *Wealth of a Nation to Be*, 109. Jones's regressions show the effects of soil and rivers on land values in the South, but she was not able to compare North and South directly. See Jones, *American Colonial Wealth*, 1742–52.

TABLE 2.4 Regional wealth in 1850 and 1860 (in dollars)

	1850		1860	
	NORTH	SOUTH	NORTH	SOUTH
Physical wealth (billions)	4,474	2,844	9,786	6,332
Value of slaves (billions)		1,286		3,059
Nonslave wealth (billions)	4,474	1,559	9,786	3,273
Wealth per capita	315	316	482	569
Nonslave wealth per capita	315	174	482	294
Nonslave wealth per free capita	315	266	482	449
Wealth per free capita	315	483	482	868

Sources: U.S. Bureau of the Census, *Preliminary Report of the Eighth Census,* 194–95; Ransom and Sutch, "Capitalists without Capital," 150–51. Free black population figures are from the U.S. Bureau of the Census, *Negro Population in the United States, 1790–1915,* 57.

course, the gains had to be shared with a larger number of individuals. But the "founding generation" of the early national era clearly had the best opportunity to capture these capital gains, by obtaining title to western lands early in the appreciation process. Recruiting new settlers was part of the plan from the start, and land values registered the success of the project.[14]

In light of these reflections, could any fair-minded observer look at table 2.3 and deny that the North decisively outperformed the South in the antebellum cold war? Well, at least one group could: the owners of slaves. Measuring economic performance in terms of population growth and land values internalizes a landowner's view of the world. Left out of this picture is the value of slave property, which after the 1790s was only relevant in the South. Table 2.4 displays the census figures for total regional wealth in 1850 and 1860, supplemented by the value of slave property in those two years as estimated by Roger Ransom and Richard Sutch. The figures confirm the dramatic growth in the value of this peculiar species of property, reflecting both the ongoing natural increase in the size of the

14. For analysis of farm settlement and the appreciation of western land values, see Stanley Lebergott, "'O Pioneers'" and "Demand for Land"; Peter H. Lindert, "Long-Run Trends in American Farmland Values"; and Robert P. Swieringa, *Pioneers and Profits.*

slave population (at greater than 2 percent per year) and the rise in value of the average slave, from $277 in 1810 to $778 in 1860.[15]

What happens when we add the two forms of wealth together? The parallelism is remarkable. As of 1850, per capita wealth was the same in the two regions, almost to the penny: $315 in the South versus $316 in the North. Because of robust advances in slave prices during the cotton boom of the 1850s, the South actually took the lead as of 1860, by nearly 20 percent. Thus, Southern slaveowners were justified in feeling that they were fully as successful as their northern counterparts in the game of wealth accumulation, if not more so; but they held their wealth mainly in the form of human property rather than land values. The forms of wealth were quite different, but each side in the cold war could declare itself the winner according to its own scoreboard.

This view of the issue pushes us strongly toward the macroeconomic interpretation advanced by Ransom and Sutch, in which slavery retarded regional economic growth by absorbing the savings of slaveowners, "crowding out" investment in physical capital—including the forms of capital formation represented by improvements in the value of land. The figures displayed in table 2.4 summarize the analysis succinctly: the average free southerner was 50 percent wealthier than the average northerner in 1850, 80 percent wealthier in 1860. But the accumulation of *nonslave* wealth by the southern economy was 40 to 45 percent below the northern standard. Slaveowners accumulated wealth in a form that had no counterpart in nonslave societies, a form that vanished when slavery was forcibly ended. Compared to an alternative scenario in which the South had been settled by free family farmers, the South was impoverished by slavery. But there was no reason for slaveowners to adopt that point of view, since even small owners were wealthy men by national standards. From a macroeconomic perspective, the matter really is as simple as that. Contrary to the oft-repeated claim that a highly developed slave economy suffered a massive setback during the war years, this analysis holds that the roots of postbellum regional backwardness are plainly visible in the antebellum data, consistently interpreted.

15. Ransom and Sutch, "Capitalists without Capital," table A.1.

Indeed, the regional divergence implied by table 2.4 is amplified when we observe that only about one-quarter of the free households in the South owned slaves, so that southern wealth was more unequally distributed than northern farmland. In turn, inequality in slave ownership carried over into greater southern inequality in the distribution of valuable real estate. Southern slaveowners were by no means a tiny elite, but were a sizeable minority with disproportionate political as well as economic influence. Those southerners who were free but not wealthy enough to own slaves were at a serious disadvantage. One consequence was that levels of schooling were lower in the South—"human capital" in more modern economic terminology—even for the free southern population, and all the more so for the slaves.[16] Because education of free persons is an intangible form of wealth, it is not included in the census figures reported in table 2.4, which therefore understate the contrast between the two regions. The South also lagged the North by such criteria as urbanization, banking facilities, and transportation improvements, forms of infrastructure investment whose significance is reflected very imperfectly in aggregate measures of wealth. To grasp the roots of these more qualitative dimensions of regional development, we have to look more closely at the relationship between labor systems and regional geography.

PROPERTY RIGHTS AND ECONOMIC GEOGRAPHY

Map 2.2 displays population density by county in 1860.[17] In the North, one sees a nearly contiguous belt of high-density counties spreading westward from New England into Ohio and Indiana, broken only by the Allegheny Mountains in central Pennsylvania. In 1860 the belt was spreading westward into Iowa and northward into Michigan and Wisconsin. In contrast, the high-density counties in the South were sprinkled like raindrops through the region. Most of the Southeast had lower densities than even

16. Ransom and Sutch, "Conflicting Visions," 280–81.

17. Maps 2.1–2.4 were originally constructed using the Great American History Machine, published by the Academic Software Development Group, version 2.0 (University of Maryland, 1995). County areas for map 2.2 are from the 1880 census. The maps were subsequently adapted for publication by Mary Lee Eggart, Cartography Section, Department of Geography and Anthropology, Louisiana State University.

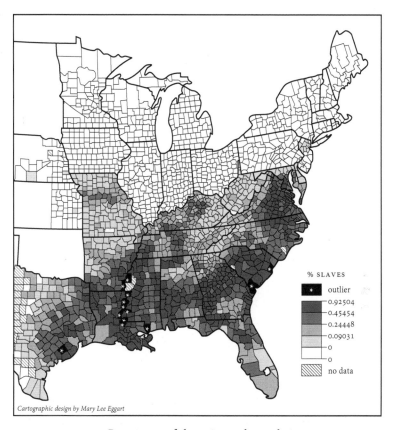

% SLAVES

* outlier
0.92504
0.45454
0.24448
0.09031
0
0
no data

Cartographic design by Mary Lee Eggart

MAP 2.1. Percentage of slaves in total population, 1860

the burgeoning frontier areas of the Midwest, a thousand miles from the seaboard starting line of 1790. The broad regional contrast in population density is well known. A view at the county level shows that this was a true regional characteristic, not an artifact of a few large cities, particular staple crops, or soil fertility. The geographic division in map 2.2 is nearly as clear as the division between free and slave states in map 2.1.

The close linkage between population density and land values is visually evident in map 2.3, which shows the value of farms per acre of farmland by county in 1860.[18] Again the regional cleavage is striking. In

18. The pattern is similar using the value of real estate per square mile for each county.

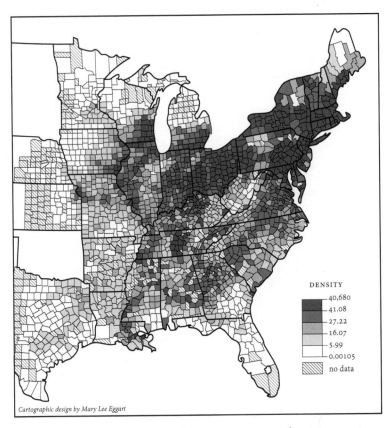

DENSITY
40,680
41.08
27.22
16.07
5.99
0.00105
no data

Cartographic design by Mary Lee Eggart

MAP 2.2. Population density per square mile, 1860

the North, variations based on pure geography are detectable, but they were overwhelmed by the development juggernaut sprawling across the countryside. In the South, not only was the overall level of real-estate value lower, but the spatial configuration was altogether different. There was no steady progression of land values from east to west, but instead several blotches of high-value lands in the Southwest, mainly along the river valleys of the Delta, but with smaller sections in central Alabama and Tennessee. These are high-yield cotton areas with convenient transportation. Across the tier of border states to the north are three high-value clusters also known for high fertility: the Kentucky bluegrass, Missouri's Little Dixie, and the Valley of Virginia, each of which featured significant

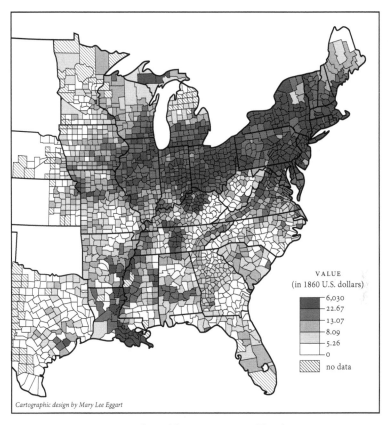

MAP 2.3. Value of farms per acre of land, 1860

concentrations of slaves. In contrast, much of the Southeast was either passed over or left behind in the process of settlement. This visual evidence confirms that however one might compare the performances of the slave and free economies, the two regional property systems had quite different geographic dynamics.

Map 2.4 displays the measure by which the South's advantage was clearest, the value of personal property per capita. Because the regional contrast is so strong, it hardly matters whether we display the total value, the value per capita, or the value per free person. These pictures look much the same, because personal property was dominated by slave values, and slaves were found only in the South. Within the South, the correlation

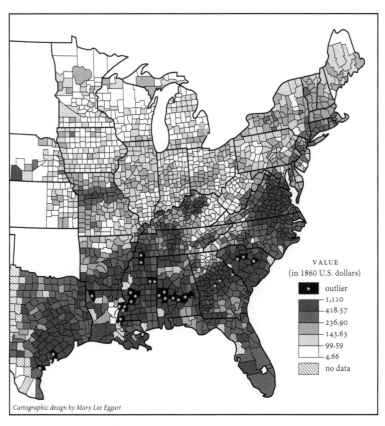

MAP 2.4. Value of personal property per capita, 1860

between numbers of slaves and personal property is evident: Maps 2.1 and 2.4 are virtually indistinguishable. The southern region may have looked underdeveloped to northern eyes, but any analysis that begins with the premise that slaveholders sacrificed wealth for class status or political power must first acknowledge that in 1860 they were doing very well on both counts. More plausibly, slaveholder politics and slaveholder economics were not in conflict, revolving as they both did around the value of slaves.

Can this remarkable difference in regional economic geography be traced to slavery? In earlier writings I developed such an interpretation, emphasizing the movability of slave wealth, the very feature that defined slaves as personal rather than real property. Movability allowed markets for slaves to function across broad geographic spaces, weakening the linkages between the accumulation strategies of slaveholders and local or regional development. Slaveholding planters were more "laborlords" than "landlords." Hence the relative underdevelopment of transportation, towns, cities, and other forms of infrastructure in the South, not merely by "crowding out" other assets in wealth portfolios, but by channeling entrepreneurial and political energies in directions that matched the processes through which asset values were determined. The culmination was the emergence of a regional political coalition whose main priority was protection and enhancement of the huge store of wealth held as slave property.[19]

This thesis accounts for the broad regional patterns, but it was framed at a relatively abstract level, and the supporting evidence was largely indirect. Fortunately, a small but growing body of subsequent specialized studies now allows us to delineate these institutional channels with greater precision.

Research by David Weiman has richly illuminated the implications of slave property for planter mobility and the land market. Although the formal structure of auctions for public lands was the same in both regions, these markets actually functioned quite differently in the North and the South. Whereas in the North purchase prices were usually at the government-set minimum (often at post-auction sales of unbid land), in the South price competition was much more vigorous, primarily because of the presence of wealthy slaveowners or their agents. Representation by specialized agents allowed a more continuous presence at these auctions and more expertly calibrated bidding. As a result, land markets in the slave South displayed much broader spatial reach than in the North. Moves by slaveowners were not necessarily more frequent than those of nonowners, but they were more calculated and more market oriented. A study by Donald Schaefer that traced individual migrants from one census year to another during the 1850s found that slaveowners moved longer average distances and with wider deviation from the principal east-west paths followed by nonslaveowners. So dominant was the influence of

19. Wright, *Old South, New South,* 17–33; Wright, "Capitalism and Slavery on the Islands."

slavery as an institution that extreme differences in the institutions for initial land distribution—such as the Georgia lottery versus the Alabama auction of the public domain—had little lasting effect on the resulting geographic configurations.[20]

Slaveowners could carry out these expansive plans because their property rights in slaves enabled them to bring labor to desired destinations at will, and because the self-contained character of the slave plantation allowed them to settle in a new area and begin production for export without extensive infrastructural support from other local parties. These "pioneers with means" had no need to adapt their work routines so as to appeal to potential migrants or to devise incentive systems in order to retain wage laborers. Instead, they simply transported the labor required to drain, clear, and improve land, and build residential and farm structures. Because of this facility for transferring whole operations, land values on the rich cotton lands of the Southwest were capitalized much faster than on comparable farmland in the North.[21]

Consider the contrast between the plantation frontier and the characteristic settlement patterns of the Old Northwest. There, most purchases were at the required-minimum family scale from the beginning (forty or eighty acres, depending on the legislation in force at the time of sale). Where larger sizes were purchased by speculators, these buyers typically shifted immediately into the roles of boosters, loan sharks, and settlement facilitators, hoping to make their profits from quick subdivision and resale. As the inveterate speculator Nathan Parker argued in his *Iowa Handbook for 1856:* "So far as speculators being a drawback to the settlement of a new country, they are the very men who contribute most to the rapidity of its settlement. Lands would be idle and unimproved for years, were it not for this class of men. They come out here and purchase wild lands

20. Weiman, "First Land Boom in the Antebellum United States"; "Staple Crops and Slave Plantations"; and "Peopling the Land by Lottery?" Schaefer, "Statistical Profile of Frontier and New South Migration."

21. Schaefer, "Model of Migration and Wealth Accumulation," 147–50. The phrase "pioneers with means" is from Cohn, *Where I Was Born and Raised,* 25. For a vivid description of the plantation frontier on the Mississippi Delta, see James C. Cobb, *Most Southern Place on Earth,* 7–28.

in vast bodies, and then make a business of inducing farmers and others in the East to emigrate hither and cultivate them."[22] Frontier interest rates were high because risks were high and credit relations poorly developed. But settler-farmers paid them anyway, because the land was initially cheap and legal title gave them the prospect of a healthy capital gain, with luck and hard work. All of these behavioral patterns were typical of nonslave settler societies, and most made little economic sense where property rights in slavery were available. None of the moneymaking prospects in such a society—hard work, a rapid influx of free settlers, or the quick buck from land speculation and/or real-estate development—had much appeal to those with the opportunity to own human beings outright.

An important component of planter mobility was the capacity to establish and maintain credit relationships across long distances, arrangements ultimately based on the asset value and liquid character of slave property. The scale and scope of the transactions could be breathtaking, as illustrated by an 1841 letter to Nicholas Biddle from a Florida planter who was simultaneously developing a plantation in Texas:

> I have mortgaged to the Bank [the Union Bank of Florida] as their security sixty slaves worth at least 30,000$, 1500 acres of land worth 20,000$, my residence near the city of Tallahasse worth 10,000$. [T]he last winter I commenced a settlement on the river Brazus in Texas where I have thirty slaves at work exclusive of those mortgaged to the Bank. I purchased there 2,000 acres of land for sixteen thousand dollars agreeing to place that number of slaves on the farm and their productive labor to be applied to the extinguishment of the debt. I understand from agent there will be made there the present year 300 bales of cotton making (?) which will nearly pay for the estate . . . My object and great desire is to relieve my slaves here from the encumbrance and remove them to Texas by the first of January 1843, and if I should be able to do so I have but little doubt the following year I shall be in receipt of between 6 and 7 hundred bales of cotton. If it is true your son is entered in a house in Liverpool this act of kindness [requested loan of $10,000] at this time may prove both to our mutual benefit . . .

22. Quoted in Atack and Passell, *New Economic View of American History,* 268. On the rapid resales by land speculators, see Swieringa, *Pioneers and Profits,* 186–227.

I shall leave here in a few days for New Orleans. Will you be good enough to address me there.[23]

In the first systematic study of the role of slave property in credit contracts, Richard Kilbourne shows that the unique liquidity of slave property served as the basis for a vast extension of collateralized credit in East Feliciana Parish, Louisiana. Loans backed by slaves were virtually risk free to lenders, who willingly maintained flexible credit relationships with planters, even across long distances and in the face of marked fluctuations in annual earnings. The same store of wealth indirectly supported another huge volume of uncollateralized credit. By contrast, land as a basis for credit was distinctly inferior, being illiquid and immobile. Although Kilbourne's study is for a single parish, his findings support the view that slavery created a strong, regionally unified credit market within the South. In this sense southern plantations constituted a more advanced and financially sophisticated form of agriculture than their family farm counterparts in the North. It is not surprising that many studies confirm the existence of effective credit-market channels in the slave South. Where such studies often go wrong is in the inference that the South was no different from the capitalist North. The institutional character of the South's financial sophistication was dramatically revealed by the severe implosion of credit that took place with the demise of slavery and the retreat to the localized, expensive, and constrained credit relationships around which postbellum economic history has been written.[24]

POLITICS, MARKETS, AND SLAVE PRICES

The price of slaves was a pervasive center of attention in the antebellum South. Slave prices were a common topic of everyday conversation and a frequent object of discussion in southern newspapers. Protecting the

23. Letter from John A. Shepard to Nicholas Biddle, Tallahassee, Fla., 24 December 1841. I am grateful to Richard H. Kilbourne Jr. for providing me with a copy of this letter.

24. Kilbourne, *Debt, Investment, Slaves*. The demise of the antebellum credit system is traced in chapters 5 and 6. Analyses of antebellum Southern banking include Larry Schweikart, *Banking in the American South*; and Howard Bodenhorn and Hugh Rockoff, "Regional Interest Rates in Antebellum America." On the highly developed infrastructure of the interstate slave trade, see Michael Tadman, *Speculators and Slaves*, 31–46, 47–82.

value of slaveholdings dominated judicial rulings in estate settlements, liability cases, and other areas of the law. References to the enormous aggregate dollar value of slave property were a standard feature of proslavery political rhetoric. For example, fire-eater William Lowndes Yancey exclaimed to a Louisville audience on the eve of the 1860 presidential election: "Again: Look at the value of that property. These slaves are worth, according to Virginia prices $2800,000,000 . . . Twenty-eight hundred millions of dollars are to be affected by the decision of this question."[25]

This characterization should not be understood to mean that slaveholders became wealthy because of asset appreciation *instead* of through the productive exertions of slave labor. Generations of economic historians have shown that slave prices capitalized the expected stream of net returns more or less appropriately (the venerable "profitability of slavery" debate), albeit with a large expectational component in these prices. Indeed, the high price of slaves created strong pressures to allocate slave labor to high-value activities. One of the frustrations in teaching this subject matter over the years is that students, even after learning theories of slavery's origin in labor scarcity and seeing the evidence of the rapid antebellum rise in slave prices, still identify "slavery is cheap labor" as self-evident truth. So, although economists will regard it as already obvious on the basis of the foregoing discussion, let me state it explicitly here to be sure: the antebellum slave South was not a "cheap labor" economy; it was a society whose economy and polity revolved around the scarcity and high price of slave labor.[26]

25. Quoted in Huston, *Calculating the Value of the Union*, 24. Huston provides numerous quotations of a similar character across the last three antebellum decades (24–25). On slave prices as a topic in conversation and newspapers, see Walter Johnson, *Soul by Soul*, 198–202. On the preeminence of slave property values in the courts, see Thomas D. Russell, "New Image of the Slave Auction"; and Thomas D. Russell, "Articles Sell Best Singly."

26. This understanding has eluded James L. Huston, who, after expounding at length about the southern preoccupation with the value of slave property, proceeds to declare that "slave labor was cheap labor" as though this proposition were obvious (*Calculating the Value of the Union*, 98; see also 89–93). The fallacy is the inference that the subsistence return *received* by the slave was the same as the market price of the slave's labor. Contrary to Huston's statement that "the effect of slavery upon the labor market depended on who owned the slave" (93), for purposes of this analysis it makes no essential difference whether the slave was owned or rented; the opportunity cost of labor was the same in either case.

And yet, the capitalization of returns imparted a certain life of its own to the interest in slave prices, as an object of both economic behavior and political pressure. Some of this attention focused on what might be called the fundamentals of the supply and demand for slaves (productivity, land sales, the African slave trade), while another portion sought to bolster confidence in the legal security and political future of the institution itself. The latter consideration helps to explain the South's confrontational posture on such issues as fugitive slaves and the status of Kansas, aggressiveness that seemed disproportionate to their objective importance for the slave economy.[27] In directing attention and energy to the value of their property, slaveholder behavior was essentially similar to that of property owners in the free states. Lincoln articulated this equivalence clearly in his speech at Hartford, Connecticut, March 5, 1860: "The entire value of the slave population of the United States is, at a moderate estimate, not less than $2,000,000,000. This amount of *property* has a vast influence upon the minds of those who own it. The same amount of property owned by Northern men has the same influence on *their* minds . . . Public opinion is formed relative to a property basis. Therefore, the slaveholders battle any policy which depreciates their slaves as property. What increases the value of this property, they favor."[28] Comparable as they may have been at this abstract level, however, policies to enhance the value of slave property were quite different from those addressed to property values in land and fixed capital.

The policy most directly aimed at augmenting slave prices was the federal closing of the African slave trade. Though this 1807 measure is commonly considered part of the antislavery agenda, having been proscribed for twenty years in a compromise between northern and southern states at the Constitutional Convention, when the deadline arrived, the South acquiesced with little objection. In fact, although the congressional debate over implementation was heated, most representatives from both regions actively favored the ban. Benjamin Tallmadge of New York re-

27. I elaborate on this interpretation in *Political Economy of the Cotton South*, 144–50.

28. Quoted in Huston, *Calculating the Value of the Union*, 149. See also the statement in a Mississippi editorial that northern attacks on slavery and expansion would "depreciate Negro property" (ibid., 55).

marked: "Since I have had the honor of a seat in this House, I can scarcely recollect an instance in which the members seem so generally to agree to the principles of a bill, and yet to differ so widely as to its details."[29]

As slave prices rose over time, proposals emerged to press for reopening the trade, reaching their peak in the radical Southern Rights movement of the 1850s. But no southern state ever adopted such a measure, and the issue was considered so politically charged that candidates for office avoided any hint of association with it. This hypersensitivity was closely tied to the awareness that reopening the African slave trade would undermine the value of slave property. As H. S. Foote of Mississippi argued in opposing the proposal: "If the price of slaves comes down, then the permanence of the institution comes down . . . the permanence of the system depends on keeping the prices high."[30]

Property rights in slavery discouraged economic diversification through another channel. In addition to the slaveholders' general interest in high slave prices, they also sought strong legal protection for their property whenever slaves were rented out to users in potentially dangerous activities, such as those on steamboats and in mines, iron foundries, and railroad construction and operation—in short the very heart of the emerging industrial economy. The legal and institutional bases for slave hiring were better developed than earlier scholars realized. But Jennifer Wahl shows that the safety of slaves had far better legal protection than free workers enjoyed for themselves. Employers of free labor had numerous devices for escaping liability in cases of injury, such as the fellow-servant rule; contributory negligence; and the assumption that risks were knowingly accepted by free workers, regarded by the law as "super reasonable" economic actors.[31] Little of this law applied to slaves, implying that slave-employing industrialists in the South, whether they purchased

29. Quoted in Mason, "Slavery Overshadowed," 64. Mason identifies the three controversial details as what to do with blacks brought illegally to America; what the penalty should be for violating the law; and federal regulation of the *domestic* seaborne slave trade.

30. *DeBow's Review* 27 (August 1859): 219. I elaborate on slaveholder opposition to reopening the African slave trade in *Political Economy of the Cotton South*, 150–54.

31. Wahl, *Bondsman's Burden*, esp. 49–77 (employment), 78–100 (common carriers). See also Finkelman, "Slaves as Fellow Servants"; and Morris, *Southern Slavery and the Law*, 147–58.

or rented slaves, had to absorb a much larger risk of worker injuries or death than did their counterparts in the free states. These risks could be mitigated by slave life insurance, a practice that spread as prices rose during the 1850s.[32] But life insurance was costly, an expense that employers of free labor had little reason to consider.

Greater concern for the safety of slaves than for free persons may seem anomalous in a race-conscious democratic society; but from an economic perspective, the disparity is simply a logical consequence of proscribing property rights in free labor. If workers retained the right to quit at any time, one could hardly expect employers to accept responsibility for the security or well-being of their employees.[33]

These drawbacks to the use of slave labor in industry would have had little economic significance if the southern employers had succeeded in recruiting immigrants to fill these positions. But immigrants largely avoided the South. Considering this possibility takes us to a core effect of slaveholder property rights on the shape of the economy. Although it is true that such urban labor as could be found in the slave South was disproportionately foreign born, slaveholders as a class had little to no interest in encouraging flows of migrants into the region. Any immigration would tend to depress the wages of labor generally, and therefore the capitalized labor in slaves. In addition, slaveowners had reason to suspect outsiders of harboring alien opinions about free labor if not indeed abolitionism.

But the primary influence of property rights on immigration was less a matter of active policy commission and more a matter of omission: Because the value of their slave assets was independent of local development (being determined in a regionwide market), slaveowners were far less engaged in entrepreneurial activity to recruit migrants to their localities, a behavior form that was all-pervasive in the free states. It is difficult to improve upon Leslie Decker's description of the northern pattern:

> The primary means by which the little operators sought to attract the settlers necessary to force up the value of the lands they owned or claimed was to use the borrowing power of precinct and county governments to

32. Murphy, "Securing Human Property"; Savitt, "Slave Life Insurance in Virginia and North Carolina."

33. See Wiebe, *Self-Rule*, 91.

finance as many desirable public improvements (schools, roads, bridges) and to attract as many desirable services (railroads, commercial centers) as possible to the land's vicinity. Thus it was that schools with capacities far in excess of the need were immediately built, that county and precinct bonds for railroads and related promotions were voted by the firstcomers, and that local debts mounted sharply during the first surge into any area.[34]

In contrast, as reported by Peter McClelland and Richard Zeckhauser, the most prosperous areas of the Southwest displayed net white *out-migration*, even during cotton booms, times when one might have expected to see a rush of immigration and development—if southern capitalism had followed the path of northern free-labor capitalism. The authors observe that "the South was continually viewed by its own inhabitants—at least by those who left—as promising less opportunity than the North. This in turn raises doubts about those accounts that portray in glowing terms the southern economic performance in the 1840s and 1850s."[35]

As this discussion suggests, the implications of activity directed toward recruiting free labor to localities and regions were wide ranging, from transportation to towns to schools, operating through both private and public channels. Not only were the laborlords of the South less likely to play lead roles in development programs, but the fixed or inelastic character of the southern labor force helps to explain why southern state politics took on a zero-sum quality, which often resulted in stalemate on proposals for internal improvement and support for industry. Two recent comparative studies of Virginia and Pennsylvania report similar reasons for Pennsylvania's more ambitious and aggressive programs. In Pennsylvania, local lobbying and logrolling meant that most major transportation and industrial-policy proposals were adopted, and areas that lost out on the first round could expect to see branch lines with relatively brief delay. In Virginia, however, the older tidewater areas (politically dominated by slaveholders) were skeptical if not downright hostile to development in the western counties and effectively blocked active state programs for that purpose.[36]

34. Decker, "Great Speculation," 378.
35. McClelland and Zeckhauser, *Demographic Dimensions of the New Republic*, 7.
36. Majewski, *House Dividing*; Adams, *Old Dominion, Industrial Commonwealth*.

The regional contrast extends even to education for the free population. Although the average wealth of the southern free population (including slave assets) exceeded that of the North, not much of this potential was allocated to investment in schooling. The spread of free common schools largely bypassed the slave South, and levels of literacy for whites were systematically lower than those in the North. Standard explanations invoke lower southern population density and consequent effects on the tax base and on the costs of transportation. But as we have seen, these elements in the setting were not dictated by nature; they were (as we say in economics) *endogenous* to property rights in slaves. Wealthy slaveholders sent their own children to private schools, but typically they had no more interest in educating poor whites than they did in developing the backwater districts. Although historians sometimes portray these yeoman communities sympathetically, as successful efforts to resist cultural domination by metropolitan elites, the implications for postbellum regional development were surely adverse.[37]

This was no more so, of course, than the absence of schooling and literacy in the slave population. But here I believe we reach the limit of the property-rights framework for explaining resource allocation in the antebellum economy. Because property rights allowed slaveowners to capture or internalize the returns to higher productivity, they actually had a greater incentive to invest in the skills of their workers than did employers of free labor. Sometimes this theoretical expectation was borne out. Charles Dew reports that the Oxford Iron Works near Lynchburg, Virginia, became a famous supplier of skilled slave ironworkers. The chief drawback to this system, according to Dew, was that the expertise of these skilled slaves tended to be frozen in time because they were unable to travel extensively and follow new technological developments, an activity their free-labor counterparts took for granted.[38] More broadly, the reasons for reluctance to teach slaves to read are too obvious to require elaboration. But these motives were not inherent in property rights; instead,

37. For literacy see Lee Soltow and Edward Stevens, *Rise of Literacy and the Common School*, 22–23, 42, 159–63, 177. For common schools, see Carl F. Kaestle, *Pillars of the Republic*, 182–217.

38. Dew, *Bond of Iron*, 79, 106–7. An earlier example of masters' preference for training slaves as forgers is described in John Bezis-Selfa, *Forging America*, 108.

they constituted external effects of one owner's actions on the interests of others. Fear of slave rebellion led many southern states to pass laws prohibiting anyone from teaching slaves to read. These laws were unevenly enforced, and some courageous slaves learned to read clandestinely despite them. But owners who actively fostered literacy among their slaves were subject to reprisals and severe criticism from their neighbors.[39]

WAS IT SLAVERY OR GEOGRAPHY?

Let me anticipate a question that always comes up. Can we be sure that these clear regional differences in spatial economy really reflect the impact of slavery as an institution, as opposed to the influence of geography, meaning climate, soils, and crops? In every generation of historians, it seems, some are irresistibly attracted to the possibility of pushing slavery out of its lead role in the story, reducing the peculiar institution to no more than an intermediate part, carrying out the dictates of deeper causal forces in the environment. Perhaps dispersed patterns of settlement merely reflected the poor quality of southern soil or intrinsic properties of southern staple crops, first tobacco and then cotton. Perhaps the immigrants who avoided the South simply found the climate or the economic opportunities unattractive. Perhaps the South had little need for transportation infrastructure because it was generously endowed with natural waterways. And so on. What can we say to this altogether contrasting, historically undramatic, yet somehow recurrently tempting view of southern history?[40]

In truth, the geographical determinist alternative has been the implicit null hypothesis throughout these essays. The reason for showing that early migration and trade were much greater in the protoslave than

39. Kaestle, *Pillars of the Republic,* 197; Cornelius, *"When I Can Read My Title Clear,"* 32–34.

40. For discussions of the South's economic geography, see Julius Rubin, "Limits of Agricultural Progress"; Douglas Helms, "Soil and Southern History." Historical geographer Carville Earle applies a variant of the "staples" thesis, in which the southern economic landscape was initially shaped by the transportation and processing properties of tobacco, while the nineteenth-century choice of labor system was driven by the seasonality of labor requirements. See *Geographical Inquiry and American Historical Problems,* 88–152, 226–57.

in the protofree regions was to make the point that these southerly areas were attractive enough at an earlier phase of history. As noted earlier, Alice Hanson Jones found that southern land values in 1774 were higher, not lower, than those in the North. When the eighteenth-century Scotch-Irish pioneers began to migrate in a southwesterly direction along the "great Wagon Road," a reason popularly given was the climatic attraction of the warmer regions over chilly Pennsylvania. One eighteenth-century observer wrote that "the migrants from Pennsylvania always travel to the southward. The soil and climate of the western parts of Virginia, North and South Carolina, and Georgia afford a more easy support to lazy farmers than the stubborn but durable soil of Pennsylvania."[41] Perhaps the image of northern farmers heading south in search of indolence evokes another venerable stereotype (of climatically determined lethargy). But by showing that North and South in the 1770s and 1780s were broadly similar in population, territory, and wealth, I meant to suggest that there was no all-powerful geographic advantage for either one over the other, looking forward from that date into a nineteenth-century history not yet known. By showing that differences in spatial configuration permeated broad regions down to the county level, I maintain that these were not mere artifacts of peculiar staples or microclimates.

To supplement these observations from the starting point of our exercise, we have the evidence of dramatic change in the geographic configuration of the southern economy at the other end of the period, when slavery was abolished. War and emancipation did not bring wealth and prosperity to the region, but almost immediately at the end of hostilities, railroads and town-building enterprises began to proliferate, and formerly isolated, upcountry areas found themselves pulled into commercial farming and cotton growing. Long-neglected mineral deposits appeared magically on the hillsides, as former slaveowners, dispossessed of their labor, rechanneled their energies into the search for capital gains on nonhuman property. New marketing centers provided processing and storage facilities, and country stores offered commercial fertilizers to small farmers, on credit if necessary. The ratio of improved acreage to rural population, which had been rising in the antebellum period, reversed direction in

41. Quoted in John Solomon Otto, *Southern Frontiers*, 49.

the 1860s, beginning its historic descent. Within one generation the region long characterized by sparse settlements and dispersed populations emerged as the highest rural population-density section of the country. With due allowance for the multiplicity of historical forces at work during the tumultuous 1860s, the case approximates a controlled experiment in institutional change. How could geographic imperatives be all-powerful if economic geography proved so malleable in the wake of a change in core property-rights institutions?[42]

Yet we do have to acknowledge the roles of geography and staple crops in regional development over the full sweep of history. That role is larger, the further back we go. Before the Revolution, slavery as an *institutional* reality did not distinguish North from South. Since the locational geography of slavery at that time was largely dictated by the presence of high-value, transportable export staples, any regional differentiation dating from that historical phase seems more appropriately linked to the staple than to the institution of slavery. As far back as we go, the pattern of dispersed settlement and an absence of towns was stubbornly characteristic of the Chesapeake tobacco regions. Following in a long line of distinguished "staples" theorists, Carville Earle and Ronald Hoffman argue persuasively that tobacco did not lend itself to towns: it traveled easily, required little processing before shipment, and generated levels of revenue relative to areas that were too low to support towns as profitable ventures. All of these effects stand in contrast to wheat, the chief northern staple. A study of the southern Piedmont region of Virginia by Charles Farmer largely confirms these associations.[43]

Even in this early formative period, however, economic geography was shaped by an interaction between staple crops and institutions. For many areas, access to transportation defined the margin of cultivation between tobacco and wheat. In the Southside region of Virginia, according to Farmer, the cost of carrying tobacco comprised one-third to one-half of the market value of the crop, whereas wheat growing was simply not

42. This paragraph summarizes chapter 2 of Wright, *Old South, New South,* "From Laborlords to Landlords," 33–47. See also David L. Carlton, *Mill and Town in South Carolina,* 1–81; David Weiman, "Economic Emancipation of the Non-Slaveholding Class."

43. Earle and Hoffman, "Staple Crops and Urban Development"; Farmer, *In the Absence of Towns.* A similar theme is in Frederick F. Siegel, *Roots of Southern Distinctiveness.*

viable commercially, because shipping costs often exceeded market value. Transportation costs were not just given by nature, but were changeable by human intervention. Because, in Southside Virginia, tobacco made few demands on the transportation system, revenues available for improvements in roads and navigation were limited, and wheat remained in the doldrums. True, we might draw a causal link between the initial specialization in tobacco and the subsequent weakness of improvements in transportation. But accounts suggest that the operative factor in the persistence of tobacco specialization was not its intrinsic habit-forming character, but slavery, specifically the drive toward self-sufficiency on the part of slave plantations.[44]

Another important allegation for geographic determinism is the linkage, positive or negative, between crops and towns. It does indeed seem that tobacco farming, whether slave or free, had little need for local processing and services. These were the demands that helped to get towns started in the open countryside. But from an early point in their evolution, successful towns broke away from the role of passively responding to demands from the agricultural sector, and converted themselves into active entrepreneurial agents for economic and political change. In their study of backcountry Virginia, Warren Hofstra and Robert Mitchell find that shipments of wheat and flour contributed little directly to the growth of towns. Far more important for an emerging center like Winchester was its role as a hub for *import* distribution to a diverse rural clientele. As Winchester expanded, its merchant community became actively involved in local land speculation and promotion, and in political agitation for internal improvements. The town also served as a way station and staging point for waves of migrants passing through, and all of these functions attracted a cluster of artisans performing diverse functions for both rural and urban customers. According to Hofstra and Mitchell, this entire scenario stood in marked contrast to the plantation section of the very same county, which traded at long distances and had little contact with Winchester. So even in this early phase, slavery made a difference.[45]

44. Hofstra and Mitchell, "Town and Country," 643; Kulikoff, *Tobacco and Slaves.*
45. Hofstra and Mitchell, "Town and Country," 636–44.

However one may read these linkages among crops, slavery, and geography, we can say with some confidence that they did not derive from compelling linkages between particular staple crops and slavery as a system of work organization. This assertion is confirmed by James Irwin's notable study of the antebellum wheat-growing slave plantations of the Virginia Piedmont. This example also has some of the features of a test case: By the historical accident of state boundaries, the plateau of central Virginia emerged as an important wheat-growing area in the 1840s and 1850s. The region was part of the tobacco belt, and tobacco was arguably a more important cash crop than wheat for the Piedmont as a whole. But as it has been throughout history, tobacco was as well suited to family farms as it was to slave labor, perhaps better. In 1860, tobacco accounted for nearly 50 percent of the total value of output on Piedmont slaveless farms, but less than 40 percent on farms with slaves. In contrast, wheat was of minor importance on slaveless farms (about 10 percent of the total value of their output) but accounted for nearly 40 percent of output value on the largest category of slaveholding units! The affinity of wheat and slavery paralleled to a remarkable degree the association between slavery and cotton further south. Yet the economic geography of the Virginia Piedmont was distinctly southern, quite unlike the migrating wheat belts of the northern states. So it does not seem that intrinsic properties of staple crops were dictating regional destinies. A property-rights explanation for this ostensibly anomalous affinity is presented in the next chapter.[46]

CONCLUSION

This chapter has two main themes: First, that the institutions of slavery and free labor had powerful impacts on the shape and scope of the southern and northern regional economies, not mainly through differences in work organization, but because of property rights. Second, that the dominant figures in southern society, the slaveowners, could justifiably

46. Irwin, "Exploring the Affinity of Wheat and Slavery"; Irwin, "Slave Agriculture and Staple Crops." The quantitative statements in this paragraph are derived from Irwin's samples of farms from the manuscript censuses of 1850 and 1860.

view themselves as winners of the cold war in economic terms, using a scoreboard appropriate to an economy with their peculiar form of wealth.

Yes, the South lacked an articulated regional city system and urban amenities; it was also short on towns, railroads, factories, schools, and universities. All of these absences had major historical consequences in the century that followed the demise of slavery. The question posed here is, did the slaveowners care? Did these *regional* deficiencies impose significant economic burdens on the slaveowning classes? It is far from clear that they did. One reason is that infrastructure and amenities failed to develop in large part because the property rights of slavery provided reasonably good substitutes—for the owners. Where they did not, slaveowners were rich enough to buy what they needed. As former U.S. Senator Louis Wigfall told British correspondent William Howard Russell in 1861:

> "We are a peculiar people, sir! . . . We are an agricultural people; we are a primitive but a civilized people. We have no cities—we don't want them. We have no literature—we don't need any yet . . . We do not require a press, because we go out and discuss all public questions from the stump with our people . . . We want no manufactures: we desire no trading, no mechanical or manufacturing classes . . . As long as we have our rice, our sugar, our tobacco, and our cotton, we can command wealth to purchase all we want from those nations with which we are in amity, and to lay up money besides."[47]

47. King, *Louis T. Wigfall*, 126.

3

Property Rights, Productivity, and Slavery

A more prudent person might decide to leave the argument at just this point. The first chapter made the case that slavery as a form of work organization has been overemphasized relative to slavery as a set of property rights, and the second chapter argued that the broad contours of southern regional economic development are best understood as consequences of property rights in slaves. Why go further? If the physical productivity of slaves has received more attention than it deserves, why add to this misallocation by giving it even more in this chapter?

My answer to these questions is that because the late antebellum productivity record has received so much attention and looms so large in prevailing thought about the economics of slavery, the task is not complete until we confront this microeconomic evidence one more time. The challenge is to show that the strong productivity performance of slave labor during this era is also best interpreted in terms of property rights. The basic intellectual strategy is this: If slavery were inherently superior as a form of work organization, these advantages should have been manifest quite generally, in many locations and economic activities. Instead, we find on close examination that slavery's apparent production advantages only surfaced in particular times, places, and activities. Interpreting this geo-economic configuration in historical context is central for the property-rights thesis. The first step is to describe that context.

THE RISE OF THE COTTON SOUTH

In the nineteenth century, slavery in the United States was closely if not symbiotically linked to the cotton economy. By 1850, nearly 80 percent of all slaves were engaged directly in agriculture, and nearly three-fourths of these worked on cotton-growing farms. But this formation was a late and in many ways surprising development in the last decade of the eighteenth century. It could not have been predicted at the time of the American Revolution, when cotton was of no commercial importance on the mainland. When a small volume of cotton exports began in the 1780s, the novelty of the source induced Liverpool customs officials to seize eight bags, on the grounds that so much cotton could not possibly have been produced in the United States. The diffusion of cotton growing became rapid in the 1790s; but even in 1794, cotton's economic significance seemed so minor that negotiator John Jay was willing to sign away the country's right to export cotton in American ships. How different would American history have been had this article been ratified (and enforced)?[1]

Textbooks traditionally ascribe this historical discontinuity to Eli Whitney's invention of the cotton gin in 1793, a storybook formula hardy enough to have survived fresh debunking in every generation. Recent scholarship makes it clear that Whitney was far from the first to build a machine for separating cotton seeds from the fiber. Roller gins invented in the Bahamas were in use on all types of mainland cotton as early as 1791, and improved roller gins coexisted with Whitney's and even extended their market for another thirty years before ultimately losing out. Whitney's gin was a genuine innovation, replacing the pinch principle of the roller with a rotating, toothed cylinder, enhancing the speed of processing though at some cost in fiber quality. But even with this element of novelty, it was only after improvements provided by subsequent machinists that the variant known as the "saw gin" achieved general acceptance from planters. The transition stretched into the 1820s and entailed mutual adaptations among growers, gin makers, and the textile industry—much

---

1. The percentage of slaves in cotton is from J. D. B. DeBow, *Compendium of the Seventh Census*, 94; the Liverpool incident is reported in Stuart Bruchey, *Cotton and the Growth of the American Economy*, 45; for Jay's Treaty, see Matthew B. Hammond, *Cotton Industry*, 21.

more an illustration of interactive diffusion than an example of a great invention that reshaped history.[2]

Appreciating the protracted character of the transition to cotton as the dominant southern cash crop leads to the realization that the process was largely driven by demand. The technological breakthroughs of the Industrial Revolution led to rapid growth of British demand for raw cotton, especially after 1785. The market received an added boost when the slave revolution in St. Domingue removed the largest previous supplier in 1792. High cotton prices throughout the 1790s generated extraordinary profit opportunities, at a time when the prospects for older staples (particularly tobacco and indigo) were bleak or worse. Lucrative returns to early cotton planters explain the concentrated interest in the ginning problem; equal if not greater attention was devoted to seed varieties, as growers experimented with seeds imported from Louisiana and Mexico. Although the exceptional stimulus in the 1790s was short term, the economic bases for cotton were more lasting. Demand for U.S. cotton grew at better than 5 percent per year down to 1860, and the South emerged as nearly an ideal cotton-growing region in the pre-irrigation era. It was said that American upland cotton could not be matched for "uniting strength of fibre with smoothness and length of staple."[3]

The geographic circumstances in cotton may have been unique. Yet the speed and extent of the supply response in the South owed something to slavery. Property rights in slaves made possible both the rapid migration of labor to the cotton frontier and the willingness of merchants to extend credit to such distant producers. Joyce Chaplin points out that most early planters in upcountry Georgia and South Carolina were Americans from other states, either with slaves already in hand or eager to purchase freshly imported Africans during the window of time (1803–7) when this was possible. She argues that slaveowners arrived with a commitment to commercial agriculture that predated the transition to cotton, to which they turned only after initial plantings in tobacco and wheat. As she writes:

2. Lakwete, *Inventing the Cotton Gin*, 21–96.

3. Gray, *History of Agriculture in the Southern United States*, 677–89; Edwards, *Growth of the British Cotton Trade*, 75–106. The quotation is from C. F. McCay, "Cultivation of Cotton," 117–18.

"Cotton did not insert these people into a commercial economy, they inserted cotton into a commercialized economy they had already constructed."[4] Although the contours of the slave economy ultimately came to resemble the geography of natural cotton-growing areas, the property rights inherent in slavery were at least partially responsible for the region's full-generation lead over the free states in agricultural commercialization.

It is often said that cotton was a good fit for slavery in another sense, in that "there are few agricultural staples whose cultivation requires so continuous an employment of labor for so long a time as does cotton." Why own the labor of a slave for an entire year for a crop like wheat, so the argument goes, when the peak labor period during the harvest extends no more than two to three weeks? There is no doubt that the length of the growing season was critical for cotton, which required at least two hundred frost-free days. But the assertion that cotton needed *continuous* labor throughout this span is mistaken. Detailed time-allocation studies report that even on the most highly specialized antebellum plantations, cotton production generally required the attention of the labor force for less than one-half the year. The remaining labor time was not unoccupied, at least not on well-managed operations, but was devoted to work on other crops such as corn, to the care of livestock, or to the countless other tasks that managers or overseers devised to keep slaves busy.[5]

There is, however, an element of truth in the linkage between cotton's labor requirements and slavery, which has to do with the crop's distinctive seasonality. Because cotton needed so much attention early in the season for planting, weeding, and "chopping" (cutting through the drill with a hoe, to space the plants at least twelve inches apart), there were typically two labor peaks during the crop year. Figure 3.1 compares the seasonality of cotton with the single-peak pattern for wheat. Although the figure is

4. Chaplin, *Anxious Pursuit*, 328. Similarly, Rachel N. Klein writes with respect to South Carolina: "The expansion of cotton cultivation helped to unify the state only because backcountry planters were already committed to slavery and eager for a new staple crop" (*Unification of a Slave State*, 268).

5. The "continuous labor" quotation is from Hammond, *Cotton Industry*, 46. My source on slave labor utilization is Ralph V. Anderson, "Labor Utilization," esp. quotation on p. 3. The classic analysis of the drive toward full labor utilization under slavery is Ralph V. Anderson and Robert E. Gallman, "Slaves as Fixed Capital."

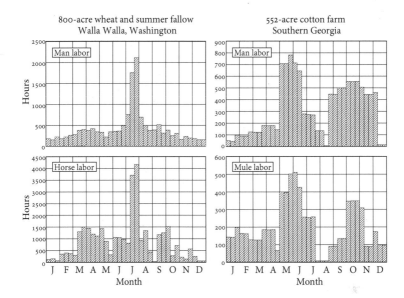

FIG. 3.1. Patterns of seasonality: cotton (Georgia) vs. wheat (Washington)
Source: Yearbook of the Department of Agriculture, 545–46.

based on data from the early twentieth century, the clear qualitative contrast reflected deep-seated features of the two crops.[6] In the Georgia farm shown, the first labor peak for cultivation actually exceeded the peak for the harvest. This aspect may have been exceptional, since it was often observed in the antebellum era that harvest labor was the constraining factor.[7] The important point, however, is that both labor peaks had to be fulfilled for success in cotton growing. It is not difficult to see that year-round ownership of slave labor had certain advantages in this regard.[8]

6. If anything, the contrast in seasonality would have been greater in antebellum times, because of the extensive mechanization of the wheat harvest beginning in the 1850s.

7. According to Anderson: "Harvest season was always the bottleneck period, especially for the inferior varieties of cotton. Total cotton acreage decisions were determined primarily by harvest season labor conditions" ("Labor Utilization," 99). For a case in which harvest labor exceeded pre-harvest labor by more than 50 percent, see the evidence for the Kollock's plantation presented by Jacob Metzer, "Rational Management," 130.

8. This advantage is central to the argument in Hanes, "Distribution of Slave Labor in Anglo-America."

These advantages were matters of property rights, not work organization or effort levels. The landowner who committed acres to cotton was taking on financial risk, and neither the planter nor his creditors would have been willing to do so without some means of assurance that labor supply for the harvest would be available. Although there are other means of achieving such assurance, none was as effective or as certain as the legal property rights of a slaveowner. Surprisingly, however, in certain circumstances slavery could be as ideally suited for wheat farming as for cotton growing, as argued below.

TRENDS AND FLUCTUATIONS
IN COTTON PRODUCTION

Supported by burgeoning world demand, cotton production in the South grew rapidly from the 1790s through 1861 (fig. 3.2). How should we understand this expansion in economic terms? Some writers proceed by simply dividing the level of cotton output by the slave population, referring to this rising ratio as productivity growth. But this practice is misleading. The *composition* of southern agricultural output was in flux between 1790 and the 1820s, as cotton replaced tobacco, wheat, and lesser crops in Virginia and the Carolinas. It makes little sense to define a productivity measure in terms of only one part of the whole. If that part happens to be rising rapidly, such a ratio exaggerates the growth of what economists normally regard as productivity.[9]

Not only were crops shifting in the older parts of the region, but the cotton frontier moved rapidly southward and westward, onto the Georgia piedmont and across to the rich calcareous soils of central Alabama and Mississippi. As early as 1821, slave-based cotton cultivation was well under way on some of the best cotton land in the world, in the alluvial bottoms of the lower Mississippi and Red river valleys, as well as the Tennessee and Cumberland river valleys in central Tennessee. Figure 3.2 shows that

9. This tradition goes back to Conrad and Meyer, who criticized Ulrich Phillips for assuming "no increase in productivity," which they then measured by dividing the value of cotton output by the aggregate number of slaves aged ten to fifty-four years ("Economics of Slavery," 116–17). A more recent example may be found in David Eltis, *Economic Growth*, 189, 287.

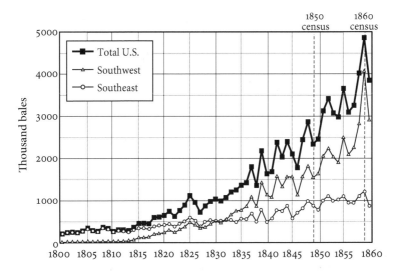

FIG. 3.2. Cotton production by region, 1800–1 through 1860–61

Source: Watkins, *King Cotton,* tables for each state.

the southwestern share of the total accelerated from the mid-1830s and was dominant by the 1850s. Thus, growth of cotton production was effected by a change in output composition, growth of the slave labor force, and expansion of cotton acreage, both quantitatively and qualitatively. Conventional "growth accounting" exercises suggest that these three factors account for virtually all of the increase in cotton output, leaving little or no residual or true productivity growth.[10]

The preceding paragraphs are not intended to disparage the entrepreneurial energies of American slaveholders, nor the efficacy of the slave system in expanding cotton production. During this early phase of economic development, it is difficult to imagine a comparably rapid response to commercial profit opportunities on the part of free family farmers. Further, research by Alan L. Olmstead and Paul W. Rhode has directed attention to the importance of experimentation and learning about biological processes for American agricultural expansion, particularly the need to adapt crop varieties and cultivation techniques to new and un-

10. See Fogel and Engerman, "Economics of Slavery," 315–16; Wright, "Prosperity, Progress, and American Slavery," 327–28.

familiar areas.[11] On these grounds, the conventional growth-accounting framework is misleading in treating the expansion of crop acreage in the western regions as though it were a mere replication of already-familiar activities.

The characterization of westward migration as a dynamic learning experience was no less true of southern cotton than of northern wheat. The critical breakthrough was the introduction of new, hybrid Mexican seed varieties, which overcame problems of "rot" and "blight" that periodically devastated crops planted with older upland and green-seed types. Only after numerous fads and false starts did a fully satisfactory variety known as Petit Gulf cotton emerge as the first true Southern standard. Petit Gulf seeds went on sale in 1833 and spread like wildfire both eastward and westward. Chronicler of cotton James Watkins asserted: "From an economic point of view the introduction of this seed was second in importance to the invention of the saw gin."[12]

The important point for our purposes is that better cotton varieties not only improved resistance to plant disease, but also raised labor productivity in picking. Extending their research on biological sources of growth into cotton, Olmstead and Rhode document the direct association between daily picking rates and the advent of "picker friendly" cottons. A great advantage of the Mexican hybrids was the tendency for many of the bolls to ripen simultaneously, the bolls opening so widely that the lint could be plucked from the pod far more easily than with any of the earlier varieties. As a consequence, standard picking rates jumped from 50 to 60 pounds per day in the early 1800s to more than 150 pounds by the 1830s. Nor were the new cottons "soil neutral," being particularly suited to the most fertile lands in the Southwest, where picking rates rose as high as 300 pounds per day by the 1850s.[13] Thus the westward migration of cotton was an interactive learning process, by no

11. Olmstead and Rhode, "Red Queen and the Hard Reds."

12. Watkins, *King Cotton*, 13, see also 74–75, 164–65; Moore, *Agriculture in Ante-Bellum Mississippi*, 27–36; Gray, *History of Agriculture*, 703–4.

13. Olmstead and Rhode, "Wait a Cotton Pickin' Minute!" Earlier accounts relating cotton varieties to picking productivity may be found in Moore, *Agriculture in Ante-Bellum Mississippi*, 46; Gray, *History of Agriculture*, 689–90.

means a mindless replication. The productivity gains were very real, and undoubtedly the pace of adaptation owed something to the commercial impulses and pressures that were integral features of American slavery. But they had little to do with work organization under slavery, because cotton picking was not a gang activity.[14]

Although the trend was strongly upward, it is evident from figure 3.2 that cotton crops were subject to year-to-year fluctuations, often extreme. Some of this variability arose from pests and blight, but in the late antebellum years, the main culprit was the weather. The rainfall and temperature requirements of cotton are very distinctive and demanding, and bad weather at any one of the critical phases of crop development could reduce yields well below potential. Even if the growth of the stalk and bolls were ideal, it was common in the nineteenth century for the fruit to deteriorate rapidly from inclement weather during the picking season. Periodically, however, a favorable growth capped by an extended period of fair weather produced a phenomenal yield, far above the norm. This seems to have happened in the Southwest during the growing season of 1859, as suggested by the dramatic production spike for that year. This exceptional performance is doubly notable, because the crop year 1859–60 happened to be the one covered by the census of 1860, to which so much quantitative analysis has been devoted.[15]

Time-series analysis indicates that the overall 1859–60 cotton yield was 12 to 24 percent above normal, this overage almost entirely attributable to the southwestern states, where yields were between 34 and 44 percent above normal.[16] These findings have been subject to some controversy, however, because neither the census nor commercial bulletins reported how much acreage was planted in cotton in those years, so we lack direct

14. Fogel and Engerman, *Time on the Cross*, 1:206.

15. One United States Department of Agriculture cotton expert wrote: "Normally, the cotton plant produces bolls the entire length of the stalk . . . It often happens, however, that unfavorable weather conditions cause a part of the fruitage to fall, and if bad weather prevails for a sufficient period a considerable portion of the stalk may become bare of fruit . . . In fact, it seldom happens that a season is so favorable that the plant is fruited from bottom to top, but when such is the case a bumper crop is the result" (Covert, *Seedtime and Harvest*, 93).

16. Wright, "Prosperity, Progress, and American Slavery," 334.

TABLE 3.1 Percentage of 1859 cotton output explained
by the relative crop year

	COTTON SOUTH	SOUTHWEST	5 SOUTHWEST STATES
1849 cotton output	2.468	1.590	1.338
1859 cotton output	5.344	4.137	3.403
1859 cotton adjusted	4.697	3.313	2.532
% of improvement 1859 due to relative crop year	13.8	24.7	34.4
% of growth 1849–59 due to relative crop year	22.5	32.2	42.2

Source: Schaefer, "Effect of the 1859 Crop Year upon Relative Productivity," 861–62.

Notes: Crops in millions of bales. "Southwest" includes Alabama, Arkansas, Louisiana, Mississippi, Tennessee, and Texas. "Southwest" minus Tennessee and Texas composes "5 Southwest States." The five-state estimate was performed in order to facilitate comparison with Wright, "Prosperity, Progress, and American Slavery," 333.

measures of yields per acre.[17] Fortunately, Donald Schaefer subsequently uncovered new evidence bearing directly on the issue, in the form of responses from county correspondents to questions asked as part of the "Social Statistics" census in 1850 and 1860. The questions were 1) What crops were short? 2) To what extent? 3) What is the usual average crop? Although these raw materials are far from ideal as statistical evidence, Schaefer was able to maneuver them cleverly into meaningful form, relying on nothing more radical than the straightforward assumption that the underlying yields followed a normal distribution. His results, summarized in table 3.1, provide striking confirmation of the time-series evidence, clearly showing that the cotton crop of 1859–60 was far above normal, mainly in the Southwest. Oddly enough, the crop year 1849–50 was below normal by perhaps 5 to 10 percent, so that the growth of cotton production between the two census years was all the more exaggerated by vagaries of the weather.[18]

17. See the exchange between Fogel and Engerman, "Efficiency of Slave Agriculture," 281–82; and Wright, "Efficiency of Slavery," 221–22.

18. Schaefer, "Effect of the 1859 Crop Year upon Relative Productivity," 854–63.

Contemporary observers raved about the extraordinary cotton crop of 1859–60. A survey of the New Orleans press cited the "fine and very favorable picking weather" as the explanation for cotton receipts "larger than ever before known." The *American Cotton Planter* of Montgomery wrote that "the picking season has been one of the most favorable ever known, especially in the Southern states." After noting that the fine weather probably improved the quality of the cotton crop as well, the writer for the *Planter* went on to marvel that "the prices have been wonderfully sustained." He concluded: "Taken as a whole, the cotton interest was never in a more prosperous condition."[19] Perhaps the unsurpassed prosperity of that season contributed to the political atmosphere of that fateful year, by enhancing the South's confidence in its economic capabilities and power. Certainly economic life was soon overtaken by political events, which helps to explain why the exceptionality of the crop year 1859–60 has been historically underappreciated.

For the more mundane world of economic history, the uniqueness of the crop year cannot be ignored. In part the lesson is merely cautionary. Of course we want to draw upon the rich quantitative resources preserved in the censuses of 1850 and 1860. But any lessons drawn must be carefully couched in historical context, both the long-term trends and the volatile annual fluctuations. In addition, there may be a more positive message from an appreciation of the exceptional character of one crop year. The capacity to take advantage of rare bumper crops highlights one of the crucial property-rights benefits of slavery: the power to mobilize harvest labor throughout the season, however protracted and however unanticipated. Many writers have portrayed the year-round character of slave labor as a kind of burden, an indivisibility that raised fixed costs and strained the manager's ability to keep slaves usefully employed. Under the right conditions, however, this fixed-cost investment in potential labor power could generate a great monetary return by allowing the owner to capture the full benefit of an abundant crop. Even in more normal years, knowing that the slave labor reserve was present made it feasible for planters to extend their acreage planted in commercial crops like cotton beyond the level that would otherwise be financially prudent.

19. Donnell, *Chronological and Statistical History of Cotton*, 164, 463, 496.

SCALE AND PRODUCTIVITY

With this historical sketch as background, we can now turn to the contentious subject of productivity comparisons in the late antebellum period. This issue has been scrutinized so extensively, and along so many dimensions, that an attempt at exhaustive review of the debate would be foolhardy. But by focusing on a small number of variables that (as will be shown) have decisive effects on measured productivity, the hope is that we can identify key relationships and thereby gain better appreciation for the workings of slavery as an economic institution. Toward this end, and to facilitate comparisons, I have tried to replicate previous research as closely as possible, beginning with the framework pioneered by Fogel and Engerman, introducing alternatives one at a time. Most of the analysis is based on data from the Parker-Gallman sample of 5,229 farms in the cotton-growing counties of 1859, drawn from the census of 1860. At some points, the evidence is augmented with data from a smaller sample drawn from the census of 1850 by James D. Foust.[20] The results are conveyed in a series of charts.

Figure 3.3 displays the main findings of Fogel and Engerman, which take the form of total factor productivity estimates for 1859 by slaveholding class and by region within the South, here labeled "Southeast" and "Southwest."[21] Total factor productivity (TFP) is the ratio of the value of output to a weighted average of inputs: land, labor, and capital.[22] The figures clearly show an advantage for slaveholding farms, particularly those

20. A description of these samples may be found in Parker, ed., *Structure of the Cotton Economy*, particularly the appendices to the chapter by James D. Foust and Dale E. Swan, "Productivity and Profitability," 58–62.

21. The figures used here are from Fogel and Engerman, "Efficiency of Slave Agriculture," 278–79. The article is reprinted in Fogel, *Without Consent or Contract: Technical Papers*, 2:241–65. Fogel and Engerman refer to "Old South" and "New South," but the geographic terms seem preferable.

22. In order to minimize variations that are extraneous to the substantive issues under discussion, all the tables use weights of .6, .2, and .2 for labor, land, and capital, respectively. These are very close to the weights used by Fogel and Engerman (*Time on the Cross*, 2:137). I have also followed as closely as possible Fogel and Engerman's procedures for defining outputs and inputs, and for dropping observations from the sample. See *Without Consent or Contract: Evidence and Methods*, 205–9.

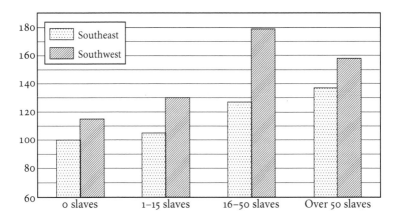

FIG. 3.3. Total factor productivity, 1860 (zero-slave Southeast set at 100)
Source: Fogel and Engerman, *Without Consent or Contract: Technical Papers*, 1:245.
"Southeast" includes Georgia, North Carolina, South Carolina, and Virginia. "Southwest" includes Alabama, Arkansas, Florida, Louisiana, Mississippi, Tennessee, and Texas.

on units with more than fifteen slaves. This conclusion holds up under a variety of sensitivity tests. Indeed, Fogel uses this very example as an illustration of the importance of doing sensitivity tests, showing the effects of various specifications of the land input on TFP. Under his favored specification, the difference between slaveless farms and the smallest class of slave farms disappears, confirming his view that the major effects arise from the gang labor system, said to be feasible only on units with more than fifteen slaves.[23]

Quite apart from issues related to defining and measuring productivity, this inference is questionable. Although it may be the case that a system deserving the name "gang labor" required a certain threshold scale of operations, it does not follow that scale was synonymous with any particular form of organizing labor. Methods of labor management were widely debated in the southern agricultural press, and many variations had their advocates. Philip Morgan, the leading authority on slave labor systems, writes that most planters devised hybrids of gang and task methods, and that many upland cotton planters "established individual tasks for virtu-

23. Fogel, *Without Consent or Contract: Evidence and Methods*, 20–23.

ally all of their operations—from plowing to hoeing to picking the cotton."[24] Writing about the prosperous southwestern cotton state of Mississippi, John Hebron Moore describes the gang system as "the old system of management," which was considered obsolete by the 1840s because it was "dangerously vulnerable to organized passive resistance by the slaves." Citing plantation diaries, Moore describes the advent of "a new system of managing slave labor," which subverted attempts at group slowdowns by assigning tasks carefully calibrated to the capacities of groups or even to individual slaves.[25] A recent essay by Peter Coclanis cautions against "attempting to idealize or reify the task and gang systems of slave labor organization," and it seems wise to heed this sensible advice.[26]

A second reason for skepticism about equating scale and gang labor is the high degree of dispersion in productivity measures around the averages for each size-class category. To convey a sense of this, figure 3.4 displays average 1859 TFP measure for each level of slaveholding from zero to over two hundred, again distinguishing the Southeast from the Southwest. One may detect a positive slope within the scatter, but it is evident that the link between scale and productivity was a loose one indeed. It is difficult to see how the efficacy of gang labor methods can be said to account for the spread of large-scale cotton agriculture and slavery, when the productivity of 30 percent of these units fell below the average for non-slave-using farms.[27]

24. "Task and Gang Systems," 199. Morgan refutes Phillips's claim that the gang system was employed on "virtually all of the tobacco, short staple cotton and sugar plantations" of the New World (189).

25. Moore, *Emergence of the Cotton Kingdom*, 78–80, 95–98.

26. Coclanis, "How the Low Country Was Taken to Task," 61–62. In recent research, Jane T. Toman also uses the term "gang labor," finding a productivity "break" at fifteen slaves in 1860. She makes it clear, however, that the system she has in mind is dividing the slave labor force into work groups according to their comparative advantage in various tasks. See "Gang System and Comparative Advantage."

27. This estimate is from a chart in Fogel, *Without Consent or Contract*, 76. The caption acknowledges that "the superior efficiency of the big plantations was due not merely to inherent advantages of the gang system but also to the concentration of above-average ability in the ownership of such farms." But of course the ability of the ownership is no more directly observable in census data than the gang labor system itself.

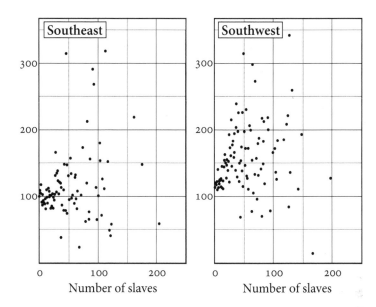

FIG. 3.4. Average total factor productivity by slaveholding class, 1860 (points represent the average TFP for each level of total slaveholding)
Source: Parker-Gallman sample.

The dispersion phenomenon has given rise to a series of technical articles in the journal *Applied Economics,* which use these data to estimate so-called *stochastic production frontiers,* allowing a distinction between "technological superiority" (the productivity achieved by the best-performing firms in a size-class) and "technical inefficiency" (the gap between actual performance and the frontier). Although the studies reach varying conclusions, they typically find that output on most large plantations fell well short of potential.[28] Together, this body of research tends to support the position articulated years earlier by Kenneth Stampp: "No sweeping

28. Grabowski and Pasurka, "Relative Efficiency of Slave Agriculture: An Application"; Hofler and Folland, "Relative Efficiency of Slave Agriculture: A Comment"; Field-Hendrey, "Stochastic Production Frontier to Slave Agriculture." See also Field-Hendrey and Craig, "Relative Efficiency of Free and Slave Agriculture." These articles illuminate important interactions, such as the importance of output composition for measured efficiency, but they do not make a persuasive case for the appropriateness of the frontier specification. Not only do

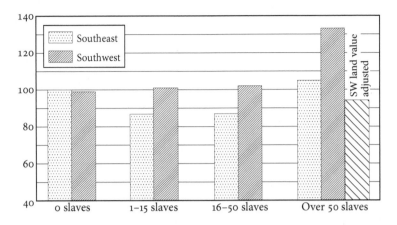

FIG. 3.5. Total factor productivity, 1850 (zero-slave Southeast set at 100)
Source: Foust-Swan sample. Output is measured by the value of crop production plus pork. Labor is the sum of free males aged 15–64, slave males aged 16–64, and slave females aged 16–64, the last category receiving a weight of two-thirds. The land input is the estimated value of improved acreage, except for the last bar, in which land is indexed by the value of all acreage on farms in that category.

generalization about the amount of labor extracted from bondsmen could possibly be valid, even when they are classified by regions, or by occupations, or by the size of the holdings upon which they lived. For the personal factor transcended everything else."[29]

A third problem is that similar procedures applied to data from 1849 (the 1850 census) rather than 1859 (the 1860 census) produce entirely different patterns. Figure 3.5 displays the results from such an exercise. It is evident that TFP differentials were far smaller in the earlier year. According to these estimates, only one slaveholding class—southwestern plantations with more than fifty slaves—generated TFP significantly larger than the base (slaveless southeastern farms). But even that one exception

---

the authors employ the term "gang labor" without evidence on labor practices, but they do not show that dispersion was mainly attributable to shortfalls relative to technical potential. It may equally well have arisen from site-specific variations in yields per acre, or from deviations from the assumptions built into the estimated variables, such as free women helping with field work (on small farms) or unrecorded off-farm laborers on larger units.

29. *Peculiar Institution,* 75.

derives from an implausibly low valuation for improved acreage in that region. When the land input is adjusted to reflect market valuations more accurately, measured TFP on southwestern plantations falls slightly below the base category, as shown in figure 3.5. My point is not to argue that the adjusted estimate is the "true" productivity measure, only to point out that these indices are highly sensitive to assumptions about the valuation of inputs.

If the apparent productivity advantage of large slave operations in 1859 were driven by superior methods of labor organization and discipline (such as gang labor), we would expect to see similar differentials in most times and places and economic activity. Instead we find that exceptional productivity under slavery was highly specific to particular locations and times and crops, and that the magnitudes involved depended critically on the values assigned to outputs and inputs. Recognition of the context-specific character of slavery's economic performance does not imply that slaves were any less valuable to their owners than was implied in the previous chapter. But it suggests that we should move away from the effort to fine-tune productivity measures so as to arrive at a bottom-line score-board ranking. Instead, it makes sense to explore the relationships among variables more fully, to see what they can tell us about times, places, crops, and slavery.

THE COMPOSITION OF OUTPUT

Total Factor Productivity indices relate two kinds of aggregates, outputs and inputs, but both of these are in actuality composed of heterogeneous elements. Some aggregation is always necessary in economics; the question is whether a specific type of aggregation has a sound conceptual basis, and what difference it makes for the results. Fogel and Engerman developed a comprehensive measure of output, aggregating all field crops at market values (whether sold or consumed on the farm), netting out assumed feed requirements for working livestock, and adding assumed annual production flows from nonworking livestock enumerated in the census. Assumptions such as these essentially represent technical relationships in simplified form, and they are reasonably standard in quantitative economics. The key *conceptual* assumption behind the analysis is

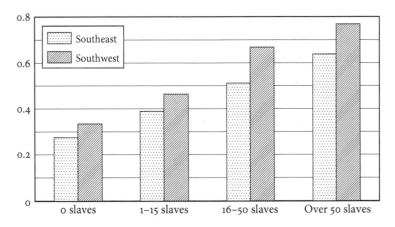

FIG. 3.6. Cotton as share of farm output, 1860
Source: Parker-Gallman sample. Definitions and prices of outputs follow the procedures in Fogel, Galantine, and Manning, *Without Consent or Contract: Evidence and Methods,* 205–9.

that farms of different scales used market-based criteria in allocating resources among competing outputs. Aggregating at market values assumes that the trade-off between one output and another (what economists call the marginal rate of transformation) was similar on small family farms to what it was on large slave plantations.

In fact, the average composition of output varied systematically with slaveholding, and this compositional difference has a dramatic effect on TFP measures based on market value. Figure 3.6 displays the pattern for 1859: the average share of cotton in total output value rose from slightly more than one-fourth on slave farms in the Southeast to more than three-fourths on the largest slave plantations of the Southwest. Thus we have the problem of interpreting a productivity difference in terms of a physical analogy or metaphor (such as workpace or technical efficiency), when in actuality the units being compared were producing very different bundles of outputs and hence were performing different physical tasks.

The market-oriented basis for allocation decisions was the feature of slavery that I emphasized most strongly in earlier rounds of this discussion. My argument was that because cotton was a cash crop while corn was largely consumed on the farm—directly by working livestock as well as by humans, and indirectly by humans in the form of pork—allocations were based on considerations of risk as well as expected profitability. Smaller farms had good reason to limit their commitment of acreage and time to cash crops, giving first priority to self-sufficiency in food, in accordance with the so-called "safety first" principle. Small-farm caution on this reading was based not so much on outright fear of starvation as concern for the financial consequences of a shortfall. Large slaveholders, having more assets and creditworthiness, could afford to take on more risk and therefore allocated resources to crops more closely according to criteria of expected profitability. But those small farmers who did specialize in cotton in 1859 (for whatever reason) enjoyed productivity gains similar to those on slave plantations, suggesting that the scale economies of gang labor were not the operative factor. Econometric evidence shows that the share of cotton in total output accounts for nearly all of the apparent productivity advantage implied by figure 3.3, and this result has since been replicated by other scholars.[30]

Fogel and Engerman's rebuttal to this critique argues in essence that the share of cotton in total output served as a proxy for farm-operator skills, introducing a kind of selection bias into the analysis: "Growing cotton was a complex task, requiring specific skills. The distribution of these skills varied at least as much among free farmers as among slaveowning farmers. Since some free farmers were more adept than others in growing cotton, comparative advantage could explain the positive correlation [between TFP and the cotton share]—although the explanation for the comparative advantage would be somewhat different in the two cases." The use of the term "comparative advantage" confirms that the analysis assumes equal marginal rates of transformation at all scales (i.e., that

30. Wright, *Political Economy of the Cotton South*, 55–74. For later studies confirming the sensitivity of revenue productivity to the cotton share, see Field-Hendrey, "Stochastic Production Frontier to Slave Agriculture"; and Field-Hendrey and Craig, "Relative Efficiency of Free and Slave Agriculture." The latter study is noteworthy in that the comparison is extended to northern farms. The authors show within their framework that controlling for the output share of cotton, mean predicted frontier revenues were higher on northern farms than on all southern farms except large southwestern slave plantations (247). Because the noncomparability of productivity indices between North and South is widely acknowledged, such comparisons do not receive further discussion in these essays.

the choice of crops was based on profitability criteria). The diagram accompanying their discussion plainly shows that the apparent productivity advantage on large slave plantations depended crucially on specialization in cotton relative to other crops. At this point it became evident that our contrasting interpretations had more to do with preferences in behavioral models than with discrepancies in statistical evidence.[31]

Although the hypothesized skill intensity of cotton growing is entirely conjectural, it must be acknowledged that the share of cotton in total output is a performance measure as well as a measure of specialization, especially in an exceptional cotton crop year. Because the census did not collect information on acreage planted in different crops (and of course we have no farm-level evidence on the allocation of labor time among crops), there is no direct way to separate these two aspects in a single cross section. At the same time, although there was great variation in these choices at all scales of operation, it is evident from figure 3.6 that the average or typical degree of specialization in cotton was systematically related to slaveholdings. If the crop mix were endogenous to slavery, then it is not fully satisfactory to explain productivity in terms of this variable, as though it were exogenous. Rather than simply declare an interpretive impasse at this point, a more constructive approach is to move away from the productivity scoreboard and explore interactions among variables more fully. If successful, we would have an explanation that accounts simultaneously for crop mix choices and for the productivity performance of slave plantations in 1859–60.

THE PROBLEM OF LAND VALUATION

Productivity calculations such as these require that a valuation coefficient be applied to the land input, because one quickly discovers that the quality of cotton land was not uniform across subregions within the South, nor across farm size-classes. Without an adjustment for land quality, the

31. Fogel and Engerman, "Relative Efficiency of Slave Agriculture: Reply," 684–85. The assumption of equal marginal rate of transformation (in technical terms, that the production function is homothetic) is acknowledged on p. 687.

1859 productivity advantage on large slave plantations (following Fogel and Engerman's procedures) would be 50 to 70 percent rather than 30 to 40 percent. So here we have another example of a variable highly correlated with both large slaveholdings and measured productivity. The question is, what does the correlation represent?

The census did not collect information on the value of particular land units, only a single figure for each farm on the Cash Value of Land and Buildings, plus the number of improved and unimproved acres. A statistical estimation procedure is therefore required, and the simplest method is to run linear regressions of farm value on improved and unimproved acreage for each regional and slaveholding class. The resulting coefficients can be interpreted as average values for each category of acreage, the value of land and buildings being captured in the constant term. These results are interesting in themselves.

Figure 3.7 treats the Cotton South as a single geographic unit and shows that average land values were substantially higher on slave-using farms than on slaveless farms, dramatically so for the largest slaveholding class. Figure 3.8 shows that this pattern was most pronounced in the Southwest. Not only was the improved acreage on these holdings four to six times as valuable as land in the Southeast, but they were also holding inventories of *unimproved* acreage that were as valuable as the *improved* land on the slaveless farms of either region. A similar exercise for 1850 generates the astonishing result that the value of *un*improved acreage on the largest slave plantations of the Southwest was higher than that of *improved* farmland anywhere else in the South.

Productivity indices are highly sensitive to assumptions about land value. As estimates of average land quality, the coefficients displayed in figures 3.7 and 3.8 are subject to bias. Very likely, lands with higher natural fertility and better location were improved earlier, so that the coefficient on improved acreage represents both geography and human investment. Even more seriously, the assumption of constant per acre values within regional size-classes was not always valid. The regressions for the largest category in the Southwest (those with more than fifty slaves) consistently generated negative constant terms, implying that the "largest of the large" plantations held land that was even more valuable than that of their

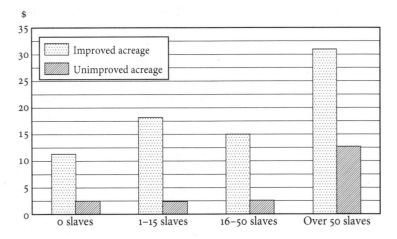

FIG. 3.7. Land value per acre, 1860 (whole Cotton South)
Source: Parker-Gallman sample. The height of each bar is derived from a regression of the form: CVF = aIA + bUA + c, where "CVF" is the cash value of the farm, "IA" is improved acreage, and "UA" is unimproved acreage.

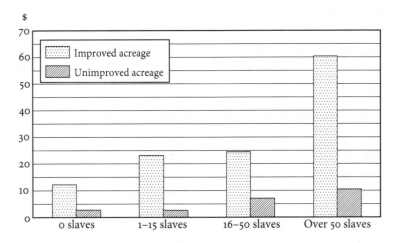

FIG. 3.8. Land value per acre, 1860 (Southwest)
Source: Parker-Gallman sample. See source note for fig. 3.7.

smaller neighbors. When the constant term is constrained to zero, the resulting coefficient on improved acreage is an underestimate of average land values on these giant units. This anomaly explains the need for a special adjustment to the land input in the 1850 productivity estimates (fig. 3.4).[32]

If our interest is solely in TFP estimates, there is no correct answer here. The available information is insufficient to disentangle the components of variation in farmland values, and we therefore cannot be certain about their productivity consequences. Because important qualitative results are sensitive to assumptions on this score—such as the productivity differential between slaveless and small slave farms—this seems a particularly weak basis from which to draw inferences about systems of slave labor management. What we can address with more confidence is the role of slavery in generating the remarkable economic geography of land value in the antebellum South.

Most agrarian societies feature an *inverse* association between the size of land holdings and their value per acre. In the slave South, we observe instead a strong *positive* relationship between plantation size and land value per acre. This evidence confirms the accounts of David Weiman, Steven F. Miller, James C. Cobb, and others about the special character of the plantation frontier, where "pioneers with means" were able to acquire at long distance and bring into cultivation large, profitable farming operations in then-remote parts of the country. The result was to drive land prices to levels that, as one contemporary put it, "deter all but Rich planters."[33] Planters could carry out these operations not just because they were rich, but because of property rights associated with slavery. Because of slavery, wealthy planters were under no pressure to subdivide their initial purchases and sell to smaller family farmers. In light of these patterns on

32. The negative constant term occurs because higher average land values on larger units force the linear regression line to swivel counterclockwise, driving the intercept below the origin. Constraining the intercept to zero is an *ad hoc* remedy, but for the largest Southwest plantations in 1850, the result is an implausibly low value of $4.11 per acre. The adjustment substitutes the coefficient from the original unconstrained regression ($15.11), which is close to the corresponding coefficient on unimproved acreage.

33. Quoted in Bolton, *Poor Whites of the Antebellum South,* 79. Miller shows that a large fraction of frontier planters arrived with enough slaves to work a plantation ("Plantation Labor Organization," 156).

the cotton frontier, it is not difficult to see why the prospect of intrusion by slaveholders was threatening to would-be settlers and developers in the free states.

THE COMPOSITION OF THE LABOR FORCE

The discussion thus far has linked the apparent productivity advantage of slave plantations in 1859 to three factors: location, the composition of output, and unusual features of the cotton crop year 1859–60. This triad might be taken as more than sufficient to end the discussion, but it is not. Both the geographic location of slaves and the composition of output were to some degree endogenous. And although the bonanza cotton crop of 1859–60 undoubtedly amplified the magnitude of the cotton-slavery premium, we should not allow this historical accident to divert our search for more systematic features of slavery as an economic institution. Figure 3.9 demonstrates the sensitivity of total-factor-productivity estimates to one other important adjustment, the application of age-sex weights to convert the labor force into "equivalent hands." The entire finding of an efficiency advantage for large-scale plantations rests on this procedure. As figure 3.9 shows, when an unweighted measure of the labor force is used (i.e., all free males and slaves aged fifteen to sixty-four, retaining the assumption that free females were not in the labor force), only the middle-size plantations of the Southwest would have any productivity edge at all over slaveless southwestern farms, and this by less than 10 percent. Clearly such a critical step in the calculations deserves more attention.

Although the age-sex weights applied by Fogel and Engerman were complex, the primary effect is to reduce the "hand equivalence" of female slaves by about 30 percent.[34] Perhaps it should not be surprising that demotion

34. The weights are graphed in Fogel, *Without Consent or Contract*, 74, and printed in Fogel, Galantine, and Manning, eds., *Without Consent or Contract: Evidence and Methods*, 206. Exactly how these weights were derived is not made clear. Fogel notes that some plantations assigned "hand" ratings to various types of slaves, though these could vary according to the task (26–27). He then writes: "An even more refined and reliable set of ratings can be obtained from the abundant data on slave prices and on annual hire rates" (73). A footnote makes reference to computing weights from the Parker-Gallman sample, but there the trail ends.

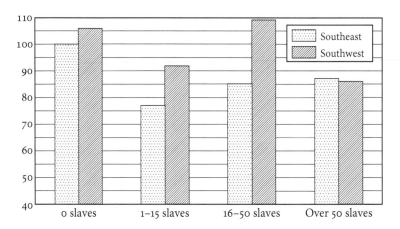

FIG. 3.9. Total factor productivity with unweighted labor, 1860
Source: Parker-Gallman sample. Variable definitions are the same as in fig. 3.3, except that the labor force is the unweighted sum of free males, slave males, and slave females from 15 to 64 years of age. The land input is the value of improved acreage, using the regression coefficients for each region and size-class, as in fig. 3.8.

of a portion of the labor input that applied only to slave-using operations should raise estimated productivity on these units. Perhaps it also seems obvious that such an adjustment is economically justified. Male and female slaves were not identical, and plantation management systems did often utilize hand-equivalent ratings such as these. Relative market price and hire rates also indicate that the value of female slave labor time was typically less than that of males. Yet we should recall that the output measures under discussion are not directly comparable physical units; they are aggregates at market value, or revenue. In a multi-product, multi-input, contingent seasonal farming operation like a cotton plantation, relative *physical* productivities lack precise definition, because male and female slaves typically did not perform identical tasks throughout the year. Relative *revenue* productivities were not fixed by human nature. And so the question arises: Why apply any fixed weights to the labor force? The further we go toward weighting both inputs and outputs by market prices, the more we convert TFP into a financial-type ratio or rate of return, as opposed to a physical measure that informs us about the workings of slavery.

These considerations suggest that there may be something to be learned by disaggregating the labor force, taking advantage of the rich detail available in the census samples. When we do, the results are surprising. Appendix tables 1–6 report coefficients from estimates of Cobb-Douglas production functions for 1850 and 1860, breaking the labor force into three components (free males, slave males, and slave females) and running the regressions separately for the major regional size-classes. Although more sophisticated econometric methods are available, this simple formulation should be adequate for the present illustrative purpose. To simplify the presentation further, the key coefficients are displayed visually in figures 3.10–3.13.[35]

For the Southeastern region in 1860 (fig. 3.10), the pattern is about what we might have expected: the coefficient of slave female labor is 73 percent of the male coefficient, roughly comparable to the relative price or hire rate of slave females. But when we look at the Southwest in that same year, we find that the female slave coefficient is actually 13 percent higher than that of the male slave. One might suspect that this anomalous result is some sort of statistical fluke, except that the differential in favor of slave women is even larger in the 1850 data (fig. 3.11). In that year, the output coefficient for female slave labor in the Southeast was 27 percent higher than the male coefficient. In the Southwest, the slave female coefficient is actually *three times higher* than that of slave males. What sense can we make of these counterintuitive results?

We can gain further insight by disaggregating the regional samples into the three slaveholding classes. The 1860 output coefficients for each type of labor are displayed in figures 3.12 and 3.13. Looking first at the Southeast, once again we find a more or less normal or anticipated pattern for the first two categories: the output coefficient for female slave labor is two-thirds of the coefficient for males on small slave farms, and just over half the male coefficient on middle-size plantations (with sixteen to fifty slaves). But on the largest southeastern slave plantations—which recorded the highest TFP levels in that region—the output coefficient for female slave labor was more than three times as high as the coefficient

35. The coefficients for free males have been omitted from the figures for clarity, and because they are statistically insignificant in virtually all cases.

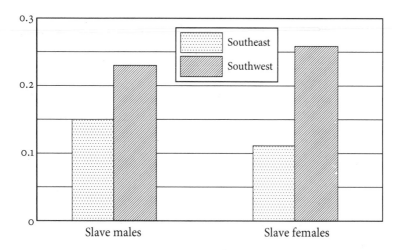

FIG. 3.10. Slave labor output coefficients, 1860
Source: Table A.1.

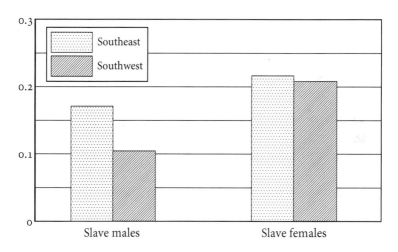

FIG. 3.11. Slave labor output coefficients, 1850
Source: Table A.2.

FIG. 3.12. Labor output coefficients by number of slaves, Southeast, 1860
Source: Table A.3.

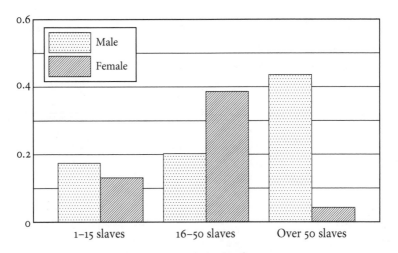

FIG. 3.13. Labor output coefficients by number of slaves, Southwest, 1860
Source: Table A.4.

for male slave labor. Evidently the apparent efficiency or scale economies of large plantations had something to do with their success at deploying female slave labor into revenue-generating tasks.

The results for the Southwest are just as striking (figure 3.13). In the smallest category of slave farms, the female coefficient is two-thirds of the male coefficient. But on plantations with sixteen to fifty slaves, identified by Fogel and Engerman as most efficient, female slaves were apparently more productive at the margin than males—90 percent more, if you take the results at face value. In figure 3.13, the largest class of plantations (with more than fifty slaves) does not fit the pattern at all. But one may peruse the regression tables for 1850 (appendix tables 5 and 6) and discover numerous additional cases in which the output coefficient of female slave labor exceeds the male coefficient, most often on the larger slave-using operations. Thus, this phenomenon seems to be not universal but commonplace, recurring with sufficient frequency to cry out for explanation.

The finding that female slaves often generated more revenue than males further discredits the notion that indices like TFP measure physical productivity performance or work effort. It would be difficult to maintain that slave women had greater overall muscular power or typically worked harder than the men. More likely, the coefficients primarily reflect productivity in picking, an activity that drew more upon dexterity and endurance than on strength. In cotton picking, average gender differentials were much less than one-third, and reports of females outperforming males are common.[36]

The critical role of picking underscores the fact that TFP does not really measure physical productivity but *revenue* productivity, in a multiproduct context characterized by overlapping seasonalities and ever-present uncertainty with respect to crop yields and labor demands. Most southern farms, large and small, maintained the goal of self-sufficiency in food requirements as a means of reducing risk and of spreading labor requirements throughout the year. But larger slave operations could extend

36. Campbell reports adult female picking rates at roughly 80 to 90 percent of the rates for adult males on southeastern plantations. Campbell also finds that women spent more days picking than men, often by substantial margins ("Gender Division of Labor," 55–69). Rothman cites a Mississippi plantation in which 80 percent of the picking was performed by women and children (*Slave Country*, 52–53).

cash-crop cultivation further for several reasons. Having more wealth, they could better withstand shortfalls in food supplies, essentially a financial risk. And because slave women were routinely assigned to field work (unlike free women), slave plantations supplied more field labor relative to the on-farm population, and hence could plant a larger cotton acreage relative to corn. Most crucially, large slaveowners could extend the margin of cotton-planting even further, because ownership of a captive labor supply provided assurance that they could mobilize a workforce sufficient to harvest the resulting crop.

Advantages of ownership and control did not pertain exclusively to slave women. But women were the most conspicuous members of the "swing" component of the slave labor force, and it is the high payoff to their efforts at the margin that the regression coefficients reflect. Reducing gender differences to fixed-weight "full-hand-equivalence" thus obscures interactions that were central to slavery's economic advantage.

The interaction between crop mix and slave female labor is confirmed in many of the Cobb-Douglas estimates, when a term representing the share of cotton in total product is entered into the regressions. For example, on southeastern plantations with more than fifty slaves in 1860, the initial estimate shows a female coefficient more than three times as large as the male coefficient. But controlling for the share of cotton in the total, the male and female coefficients are virtually identical (appendix table 3). In cases like this, the female-slave variable does the work of the crop-mix variable, statistically speaking. Economically speaking, the two effects should be seen as jointly determined. Similar interactions may be observed in appendix tables 3, 4, 5, and 6. The effect does not operate in the same way in every case. But we would not expect it to be an invariant relationship, bearing in mind that it derives in part from responses to fluctuations in crop yields. Given the limitations of census data, we have no way to distinguish anticipated from unanticipated success in cotton growing a priori. But property rights in slave labor, especially in women, were key to success in either case.[37]

37. In an ingenious econometric approach, Jane T. Toman uses a translog production function framework to estimate the Euclidean length of a "ray" to the origin from any point on the cotton-corn transformation curve. Her results strikingly confirm that the productivity advantage of large plantations (those with more than six prime-age male slave equiva-

ANOTHER ILLUSTRATION:
SLAVERY AND WHEAT IN VIRGINIA

Perhaps the best way to demonstrate that the linkage between commercial agriculture and family labor was a basic economic feature of slavery is to show that similar relationships prevailed when we observe slavery in a very different geographic setting, far removed from the Cotton Belt.[38] It may surprise many readers to learn that slavery could flourish in prime wheat-growing areas, but this conjunction was familiar to residents of the Valley of Virginia, the largest and easternmost of the border-state clusters of high-value farmland and slave population. Farmers considered its superior limestone soils ideal for growing wheat, easily the leading cash crop of the valley. The district was, after all, home to Cyrus McCormick, inventor of the reaper, whose father operated a slave-using wheat farm in Rockbridge County. Slavery was by no means incompatible with the Valley's mixed farming menu of wheat, corn, oats, hay, and diverse livestock.[39]

Indeed, in a microeconomic study focused on the Virginia Piedmont area just to the east (but within the cluster in maps 2.1 and 2.3), James Irwin reports that slavery and wheat were intimately linked within the area. He found large slaveholding units (in this area, "large" means those with twenty or more slaves) significantly more specialized in wheat production than smaller farms nearby, wheat evidently occupying a cash-crop niche similar to that of cotton across the larger expanse of the South. The positive association is displayed in figure 3.14, contrasted with the inverse relationship between tobacco and the size of slaveholding. If anything, the divergence between large and small operations increased during the 1850s. Wheat amounted to barely 10 percent of total farm output on slaveless farms in 1860, while tobacco constituted nearly 50 percent of their output in that year. This evidence thus confirms the absence of a

---

lents, roughly equivalent to fifteen total slaves) was primarily attributable to the increase in the marginal productivity of female slaves. See "Gang System and Comparative Advantage," tables 3 and 4.

38. This section draws upon Wright, "Slavery and American Agricultural History," 536, 541–48.

39. The success of the Valley farm economy, and the integral place of slavery within it, is confirmed by several studies collected in Koons and Hofstra, eds., *After the Backcountry.*

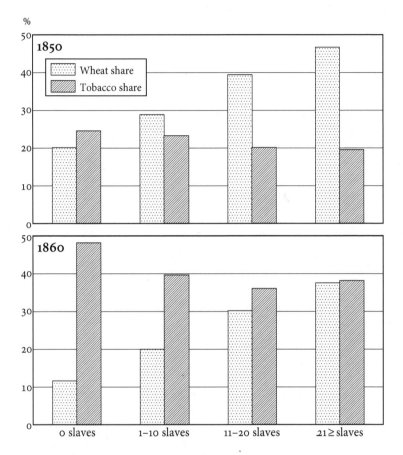

FIG. 3.14. Shares in total farm output by number of slaves,
Virginia Piedmont, 1850 and 1860

Source: Irwin sample. Following Irwin, total output is the sum of crop production
at market value, plus estimates of the net value of mutton, beef, and pork.

distinct production-based association between tobacco and slavery. Since tobacco is the very prototype of a care-intensive crop, a last bastion of the small family farm long after the demise of slavery, this news is hardly surprising. But it intensifies the puzzle of explaining the apparent affinity between wheat and slavery on the Virginia Piedmont.[40]

Perhaps it is appropriate to begin with the feature of wheat-farming most often thought to be unsuited to slave labor: the strong seasonality of labor requirements, as depicted graphically in figure 3.1. Surely it would be inefficient to solve the peak-labor problem by buying and holding a stock of slave laborers for an entire year just to cover the labor requirements of a single month. Indeed it would, but this was not standard practice. Documentary evidence from the Lower Shenandoah Valley decisively refutes the contention that slaves on wheat farms were underemployed for significant portions of the agricultural year. According to detailed work diaries surveyed by Kenneth W. Keller, "slaves were employed at all seasons of the year in a variety of arduous tasks":

> Slaves' work included laying off new fields; removing stones from the fields and hauling them away; cutting trees and hauling wood to town, to the railroad depot, or to sawmills; harrowing; scraping manure from barnyards; hauling, plowing and spreading gypsum and manure; sowing; constructing and maintaining log and stone fences to keep cattle out of the fields; harvesting and threshing wheat; cleaning, sowing, threshing, and hauling clover that was used to replenish nitrogen in the wheat fields; stacking wheat; repairing wheat stacks; cleaning and screening wheat; hauling wheat to the mill; hauling wheat straw, fodder, and chaff; burning straw and chaff; preparing seed wheat; cutting clover grown in the wheat fields after the harvest; and foddering the cattle. Once these chores were done, slaves did not rest. There was coal to haul; ice to cut and load; beef and mutton to salt; and corn to plant, thin of shell. Other slave tasks included bringing loads of gypsum or buckwheat; shucking corn; pounding hominy; planting and tending gardens; digging out hotbeds; planting and digging potatoes; patching bags; making shingles; making butter and cheese; bury-

40. Irwin, "Exploring the Affinity of Wheat and Slavery." Figures 3.14 and 3.15 draw upon Irwin's samples from the manuscript census. I am grateful to Professor Irwin for sharing his data with me. For details on his procedures, see Irwin, "Slave Agriculture and Staple Crops."

ing cabbage or beets; repairing cisterns; sheering sheep; tending livestock; greasing and oiling harnesses; working on roads; making currant wine; mowing; cutting oats; and working on neighboring wheat farms, if one's master lent or hired out his labor force to a neighbor.[41]

To acknowledge the obvious: much of the diversity of tasks on this list reflected the mixed character of farming in Virginia, including both the variety of cash products and the mix of market and nonmarket activities. Further, the heterogeneity of the tasks undoubtedly set limits on the feasible scale of farming operations. But although magnitudes varied, the principles at work did not differ fundamentally from those in the Cotton Belt, where farms also strove for maximum self-sufficiency and found numerous ways to fill out the work year productively. The important point is that these adjustments were indeed possible under slavery, even in a farming area whose geography, soils, and crops contrasted so strongly with those of the Deep South. Slavery was firmly entrenched in the antebellum Virginia wheat economy on the eve of the Civil War.

This discussion explains why slavery and wheat were not *in*compatible partners; but how then should we understand the positive association between the two on the Virginia Piedmont? In careful econometric work, Irwin rejects the hypothesis that the answer lay primarily in scale-dependent trade-offs between wheat and other crops, i.e., a shift of inputs along a farm-level transformation curve. Wheat-planting clearly had an opportunity cost in land use, in that the same acres could not be planted in tobacco or other crops; but Irwin finds that other input requirements dovetailed well with those for wheat, so the affinity was not mainly a matter of sacrificing other products. Citing descriptions of finely tuned harvest teams, Irwin inclines toward an explanation based on the superior efficiency of large-scale operations, especially the pace and effectiveness of harvest labor.[42]

41. Keller, "Wheat Trade on the Upper Potomac," 27. Wheat planters in Tidewater Virginia also made effective year-round use of their slaves. Drawing upon the journal of slave-owner John Walker, Claudia Bushman writes: "While historians have considered slave labor inefficient for grains, Walker kept his hands busy throughout the year . . . Through all seasons of the year, Walker drove his slaves with a steady agenda of work" (*In Old Virginia*, 34). The classic statement of this principle is Anderson and Gallman, "Slaves as Fixed Capital."

42. Irwin, "Exploring the Affinity of Wheat and Slavery," 302, 304–15.

There are several reasons to look beyond an answer couched solely in terms of generalized productive efficiency. Scale effects in wheat production per se are not clearly supported by the data, and Irwin is careful to note that other interpretations are possible. As with cotton, total factor productivity calculations are highly sensitive, both to the weights assigned to various components of output and to the weighting of different members of the labor force—men, women, and children across the full range of ages. Considering the entire farming enterprise as a package of heterogeneous inputs and outputs (as suggested by the list of tasks quoted above), we may question whether labor performance in one specific phase of one particular crop does justice to the larger picture.

A first step in an alternative explanation is suggested by returning to the affinity between slavery and high-valued farmland. Figure 3.15 displays the average values of improved acreage on the four classes of slaveholding farms. It is evident that the same positive association found in the Cotton South also prevailed on the Virginia Piedmont. The differences were not small: in 1850 the value per improved acre on the largest slaveholding units was more than double the value on slaveless farms, and by 1860 the ratio had climbed to 2.5. If the differences in land value reflected differences in average crop yields, we can understand the difficulties that small and slaveless farms faced in cultivating wheat as a cash crop. Their expected yields per acre may not have been high enough to justify the expense and risk entailed in planting an extensive acreage in wheat.

Our task is not yet complete, unless we can also explain why high-valued wheat lands were primarily in the hands of slaveowners. As in the cotton areas, one should not conceive of this correlation either as the accidental result of a favorable endowment or as the direct exercise of political influence. An interpretation rooted in property rights is implicit in the foregoing discussion. As suggested by Hanes's thesis linking slavery and turnover costs, slaveholding farms could accept the risks of extensive wheat-planting because they possessed a captive labor force that they knew would be available for the peak harvest demand. And, they could extend this risk-taking that much further because social norms concerning women and children did not constrain their assignments of tasks to slaves. As one ex-slave recalled: "John Fallons had 'bout 150 servants an' he wasn't much on no special house servants. Put everybody in de field,

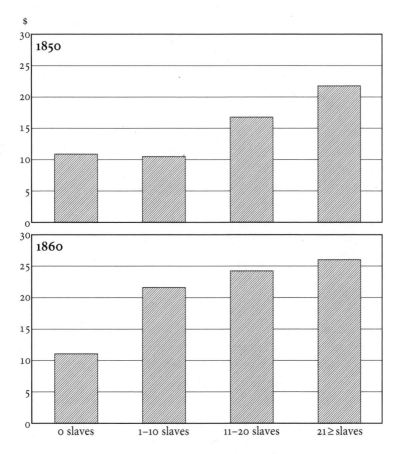

FIG. 3.15. Land value per acre by slaveholding class,
Virginia Piedmont, 1850 and 1860

Source: Irwin samples. Values are derived from regressions of the cash value of farms on improved and unimproved acreage. To avoid upward bias, the regressions were constrained to run through the origin.

he did, even de women. Growed mostly wheat on de plantation, an' de men would scythe and cradle while de women come along an' stack." The contrast between this description and harvest labor in the free states could hardly be sharper. In the North, not only was harvest labor (and field work generally) reserved for men by social convention but farmers were more concerned with the brute challenge of recruiting and retaining hired labor of any kind than with the detailed specification of harvest tasks. Thus, on his trips to the Ohio Valley, Cyrus McCormick wrote home to Virginia "of crops wasting for lack of labor to harvest them."[43]

If property rights in slaves facilitated commercialization in wheat-farming, the mention of McCormick's name calls attention to one of the long-term implications of the contrast in labor systems. Under slave-based mixed farming, labor requirements dovetailed across tasks to fill out the work year—or were adjusted to do so. But in the states where profit opportunities in wheat were favorable but slavery was prohibited, powerful pressures built to solve the peak-labor problem through mechanization. These incentives were well understood by McCormick, who largely abandoned the Virginia market after 1845, moving his reaper business permanently to Chicago, where it prospered during the wheat boom of the 1850s. Using the language of development economics, the mere *invention* of the reaper would have been of relatively small consequence unless coupled with purposeful *development* and *diffusion* of the invention. Together, these processes constitute economic *innovation,* one of the driving forces behind long-term productivity growth. But these processes mainly occurred in the northern states.[44]

In support of this interpretation, consider the cross-section pattern of farm implements per worker in the Virginia Piedmont, as shown in figure 3.16. In 1850 farm implements per workers were distinctly lower on farms with slaves than on farms without slaves. By 1860 the downward slope was diminished, as farms of all sizes increased their use of implements, and the ratios were roughly constant across classes. In conjunction with

43. Hanes, "Distribution of Slave Labor in Anglo-America"; Perdue, Barden, and Phillips, eds., *Weevils in the Wheat,* 26; Hutchinson, *Cyrus Hall McCormick,* 208–9.

44. Fleisig, "Slavery, the Supply of Agricultural Labor, and Industrialization," 573–74, 585–90.

TABLE 3.2 Value of implements and machinery/labor, 1860 (in dollars)

| REGION/STATE | IMPROVED ACREAGE | | | | |
	0–24	25–49	50–99	100–199	200 AND OVER
Illinois	10.91	28.09	51.81	75.19	125.00
Indiana	10.28	26.81	44.25	72.46	120.48
Iowa	8.77	26.60	39.84	62.50	111.11
Kansas	10.52	25.32	40.32	66.67	250.00[a]
Michigan	8.20	21.28	36.23	50.25	
Midwest	9.87	26.11	47.39	74.63	125.00
Northwest	9.48	26.32	45.87	72.99	120.48
Ohio	7.05	29.07	49.50	79.37	111.11[a]
Wisconsin	11.29	28.65	50.51	71.94	109.89

Source: Bateman-Foust sample.

Note: "Labor" defined as males, aged fifteen to sixty-four.

[a] Less than five cases.

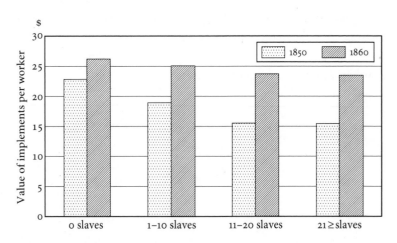

FIG. 3.16. Farm implements per worker, Virginia Piedmont, 1850 and 1860
Source: Irwin samples.

figure 3.14, the evidence in figure 3.16 firmly rejects the possibility that the affinity between wheat and slavery was driven by greater mechanization on large slave-using farms. Contrast this pattern with table 3.2, which reports data from the 1860 manuscript census, showing a strong positive relationship between farm size and the value of implements per worker in the northern states.[45]

In the free states, mechanization allowed family farmers to avoid the risks and hassles of dealing with unreliable nonfamily labor and thus enabled them to expand the scale of their farming operations in a sustainable manner. On this reading, the contrast in regional technologies had little if anything to do with shortcomings of slavery as a form of work organization, or with the inability of slaves to master skilled tasks. Instead, property rights in machines offered a free-state alternative to property rights in labor. One local historian, writing in 1955, recognized this inverse relationship by speculating:

> Perhaps the supply of slave labor, which included experienced and expert cradlers, explains the absence of the machine even on the best farms. The art of cutting wheat with a cradle was known to older men remembered by this generation, and it was not an uncommon sight, as late as thirty to thirty-five years ago to see fields of wheat harvested with cradles, although binders had come into general use then, and custom harvesting was the prevailing practice, as it had been since the latter part of the nineteenth century. In addition to men skilled in the use of the cradle, there were men and women who were also skilled in tying the bundles of grain cut and dropped by the cradler and who followed him as he made his rounds.[46]

The adaptation of slavery to wheat-farming, therefore, carried the implication that Virginia agriculture was largely isolated from what became the mainstream of technological progress and productivity growth in American agriculture.

45. Table 3.2, which draws upon the Bateman-Foust sample, was first presented in Wright, *Political Economy of the Cotton South,* 54. As noted in the preface to that book, I am grateful to Jeremy Atack for assistance in compiling the table.
46. Bradshaw, *History of Prince Edward County, Virginia,* 342.

SUMMING UP

The preceding sections may appear to be a complex series of propositions on diverse issues, but they may be summarized concisely: The economic advantages of slavery (to owners) and the apparent productivity performance of slave labor in the antebellum era may be attributed more aptly and consistently to property rights than to work organization and physical efficiency. Although a full list of relevant property-rights features of slavery would be much more lengthy, these essays have highlighted three:

1. Slavery and the Land Market. Ownership allowed planters to transport labor readily to distant and ofttimes undesirable locations and promptly to set about clearing the land. These capabilities in turn facilitated economic calculation and flows of capital at long distance, enabling planters to obtain and maintain large holdings of the most fertile farmland in the region.

2. Family Labor Allocation. Owners could override the preferences and family responsibilities of their slaves, assigning them to any tasks in any season of the year. Thus slaveowners could extract much more labor from households than these households would voluntarily have supplied. Or to put the matter more appropriately in historical context, slaveowners could reallocate family labor from household or nonmarket activities into cash crops, using profitability criteria.

3. Peak Labor and Commercialization. Because they possessed a captive labor force, slaveowners could extend the planting and cultivation of cash crops without risk that harvest labor would fall short of peak requirements. Not only did their property rights enable planters to avoid downside risk, but they were in position to take advantage of potential returns in years of exceptional crop yields, such as the census year 1859–60.

These features of slavery influenced economic dynamics as well as static productivity comparisons. Property rights in slaves facilitated rapid development of the best farmland and commercialization of agriculture, giving the South an early economic lead. Over time, however, the dynamic progress of migration, infrastructure, and technology in the free states far exceeded the expectations of eighteenth-century observers, leaving the South behind on the path to modern economic development.

EPILOGUE

The Legacy of Slavery

Judging a book by its title, some readers may have expected to find here an account of the contribution of slave labor to American economic growth, a topic that has received much attention from legal scholars and advocates in recent years. It is undeniable that enslaved African Americans supplied a substantial portion of the labor that built the American economy, and that they were not fairly compensated for their exertions. Despite its significance, this historical injustice is not the central concern of this book. These essays have dealt instead with the role of *slavery* as an institution—specifically as a set of property rights possessed by slaveowners and unavailable to landowners and employers of labor in the free states—in U.S. economic development in the nineteenth century. At an earlier historical phase, slave-based commerce played an integral role in the rise of the Atlantic economy, and thus indirectly fostered progress in the mainland colonies of North America as well. But by the end of the eighteenth century, a global shift of economic activity toward temperate-zone regions was well under way, and the development of these parts of the United States was decisively shaped by their drive to attract free labor. Thus it was not slavery but the post-Revolutionary War abolitions and the exclusion of slavery from the Northwest Territory that launched the American economy on its modern trajectory.

Contrary to depictions of the slave South as a prosperous economy devastated by war and abolition, these essays locate the roots of postbellum regional backwardness firmly in the antebellum era. That era was prosperous indeed for the slaveowners. But if we evaluate regional performance using a consistent measuring rod appropriate for a free society, such as the value of nonslave wealth per capita, we find levels in the South just over half those in the free states. And these ratios understate the regional gap, because they neglect investments in education ("human capital" in conventional economic terminology) that would be part of a more comprehensive definition of nonslave wealth. From this perspective, the postwar North-South disparity of roughly two-to-one in per capita income, a persistent feature of the U.S. economy between the Civil War and World War II, was basically consistent with prewar patterns.

To be sure, by global standards the antebellum South was not one of the truly impoverished or backward economies of its day. By such indicators as railroad mileage, agricultural technology, banks, and even manufacturing, the South of 1860 was above the world average, and far ahead of Brazil, to name another large slave-based economic nation. But much has been made of the claim that the 1860 southern economy would have been the fourth richest in the world had it been an independent nation. In contrast, using more meaningful and less volatile wealth measures, the region would come in no better than fifteenth on a world scale, about the same as in postbellum years. Such international league tables are by no means precisely defined or measured, but they confirm that in broad economic terms the antebellum South is appropriately grouped with the middling countries of that era, such as Spain, Austria, Norway, or Portugal.[1]

In many respects, however, framing the issue as a calibration of the regional economy's developmental level is not a satisfactory way to assess the economic legacy of slavery. For one thing, although these essays attribute southern underdevelopment to slavery uncompromisingly, the region's postbellum economic history need not be seen as an inevitable consequence of the peculiar institution. Societies sometimes recover

1. The comparison with Brazil is from Richard Graham, "Slavery and Economic Development." Alternative estimates of GDP per capita may be found in Leandro Prados de la Escosura, "International Comparisons of Real Product," 24–32. Prados's estimates, which use a proxy for Purchasing Power Parity procedures, differ considerably from the more standard figures developed by Angus Maddison. The differences, however, have virtually no bearing on the rank of the South in 1860.

rapidly from wartime destruction, and sweeping institutional restructuring can be a positive benefit in economies otherwise well positioned for economic development. Germany and Japan after World War II are oft-cited examples. More directly to the point, the post–Civil War South *did* in fact experience a significant economic invigoration on many fronts, including railroad investment, town-building, minerals-based industrial development, and a vigorous cotton textile industry that by the end of the century challenged New England for supremacy in the national market.[2] The abolition of slavery constituted an authentic institutional revolution, and if the New South had delivered on its rhetorical promise of sustained prosperity for the region as a whole, the legacy of slavery might have quickly receded into the mists of historical memory. This is not the place to recount this history of early promise and subsequent disappointment. Suffice it to say that the postbellum South's economic road had many forks, which deserve analysis on their own historical terms rather than perfunctory dismissal as aftereffects of slavery.

Yet it would require either epic obtuseness or willful denial to overlook the historical linkages between slavery and the political-economic regime that came to define the South by the end of the nineteenth century. White southerners accepted black participation in politics and access to schools only so long as these policies were enforced by federal authority. The intensity of racial feeling that underlay disfranchisement and segregation surely owed much to the two centuries of race-based slavery that came before. And as southern politics unfolded during the bleak *fin de siècle* period, power fell disproportionately into the hands of wealthy planters, whose position at the top of the economic hierarchy (or that of their forebears) was directly attributable to slavery. James Oakes argues persuasively that the crystallization of planters as a politically conscious class was more advanced in the early twentieth century than it had been under slavery.[3] Yet this consolidation could only have occurred in conjunction with ownership of vast plantations descended from antebellum times, made possible in turn by the property rights of slaveowners, as argued in these essays.

2. See Wright, *Old South, New South,* 33–50, 129–46. The case for institutional demolition as economic stimulus was most famously articulated by Mancur Olson, *Rise and Decline of Nations.*

3. "Present Becomes the Past."

Perhaps the most enduring legacy of slavery, then, was the persistence of a bifurcated society in which economic elites did not identify with or internalize the well-being of the majority of the population. As dramatically different as southern economic structures were between the antebellum and postbellum eras—and these changes were fundamental—this feature is a unifying thread. Taking a long historical view, true identification between elites and lower orders may be more the exception than the rule. But the South stands out in American history because with rare exceptions its propertied classes were not called upon to attract and retain a labor force through positive economic and political incentives. Before the war, property rights in slaves left owners indifferent or hostile to investments in social infrastructure and schooling, policies that elsewhere were critical in recruiting immigrants and extending democracy. After the war, African Americans experienced a sharp increase in literacy during their first generation of freedom. But with the end of Reconstruction, wealthy planters allied with other whites to deny blacks the vote, disfranchising large numbers of poor whites in the process—a not altogether unintended byproduct. Perhaps the most important economic consequence of this antidemocratic political revolution was chronic underinvestment in schooling, particularly for blacks but also for many southern whites. Unequal and underfunded southern schools were thus a legacy of slavery, as well as an integral aspect of persistent regional economic backwardness.[4]

Even when the South began its surge to economic modernity during and after World War II, progress took a noninclusive form that mirrored the region's undemocratic politics. African Americans in particular were alienated to such an extent that more than four million of them departed for other parts of the country between 1940 and 1970, the very decades

4. On black disfranchisement and its effects on poor whites, see J. Morgan Kousser, *Shaping of Southern Politics*; and Michael Perman, *Struggle for Mastery*. On the consequences for education, see Robert A. Margo, *Race and Schooling*; and Pamela Barnhouse Walters, David R. James, and Holly J. McCammon, "Citizenship and Public Schools." Linkages among labor recruitment, extension of the franchise, and schooling are stressed by Stanley L. Engerman and Kenneth L. Sokoloff, "Evolution of Suffrage Institutions in the Americas." A recent growth-accounting analysis confirming the role of poor education for southern economic backwardness between 1880 and 1950 is Michelle Connolly, "Human Capital and Growth in the Postbellum South."

when southern per capita incomes were converging on national norms. The Civil Rights revolution of the 1960s went a long way toward overthrowing this historical legacy of slavery, reversing the flow of black migration and opening new opportunities to previously excluded groups. But since that time the country has relapsed quite far into an economic culture of bifurcation and dualism. We Americans must ask ourselves how well we will honor the legacy of emancipation in the twenty-first century.

APPENDIX

TABLE A.1 Cobb-Douglas production functions, 1860

	SOUTHEAST		SOUTHWEST	
	(1)	(2)	(3)	(4)
Constant	0.42	1.24	1.34	0.47
	(1.1)	(3.6)	(3.2)	(1.4)
Value of implements and machinery	.381	.262	.297	.313
	(5.8)	(4.5)	(5.6)	(7.2)
Value of improved acreage	.448	.356	.372	.355
	(8.1)	(7.2)	(7.5)	(8.7)
Free males	.035	.081	-.075	-.041
	(0.6)	(1.7)	(1.6)	(1.0)
Slave males	.152	.206	.228	.171
	(3.0)	(4.5)	(4.6)	(1.0)
Slave females	.111	.094	.258	.182
	(2.2)	(2.2)	(4.9)	(4.2)
Share of cotton in output		1.48		1.58
		(25.7)		(21.1)
R^2	.642	.705	.608	.736
N	629	629	918	918

Note: Dependent variable: ln value of crop outputs plus pork. Figures in parentheses (in table body) are t-ratios.

TABLE A.2 Cobb-Douglas production functions, 1850

| | SOUTHEAST | | SOUTHWEST | |
	(1)	(2)	(3)	(4)
Constant	2.62	2.27	3.77	4.03
	(6.8)	(7.0)	(13.0)	(17.2)
Value of implements and machinery	.137	.129	.152	.120
	(3.2)	(3.6)	(4.5)	(4.3)
Value of improved acreage	.457	.425	.318	.204
	(7.5)	(8.3)	(6.4)	(5.0)
Free males	-.021	-.005	.041	.006
	(0.3)	(0.1)	(0.6)	(0.0)
Slave males	.171	.105	.114	.129
	(2.6)	(1.9)	(1.7)	(2.4)
Slave females	.217	.208	.350	.286
	(3.3)	(3.8)	(5.3)	(5.4)
Share of cotton in output		1.25		1.45
		(7.7)		(12.2)
R^2	.821	.875	.749	.836
N	146	146	282	282

Note: Dependent variable: ln value of crop outputs plus pork. Figures in parentheses (in table body) are t-ratios.

TABLE A.3 Cobb-Douglas production functions, 1860
(Southeast by slaveholding class)

	1–15 SLAVES		16–50 SLAVES		OVER 50 SLAVES	
	(1)	(2)	(3)	(4)	(5)	(6)
Constant	1.89	2.49	0.47	1.04	1.63	-0.12
	(4.0)	(5.9)	(0.8)	(1.9)	(0.8)	(0.1)
Value of implements	.181	.096	.136	.105	-.185	-.001
and machinery	(4.3)	(2.5)	(2.3)	(1.9)	(1.2)	(0.0)
Value of improved	.458	.348	.689	.560	.726	.647
acreage	(6.9)	(5.9)	(8.5)	(7.0)	(3.0)	(3.8)
Free males	.046	.110	.127	.129	-.424	-.111
	(0.6)	(1.7)	(1.4)	(1.5)	(2.1)	(0.7)
Slave males	.185	.216	.183	.239	.125	.175
	(2.6)	(3.5)	(2.0)	(2.8)	(0.4)	(0.9)
Slave females	.123	.113	.094	.078	.406	.176
	(1.7)	(1.8)	(1.0)	(0.9)	(1.7)	(1.0)
Share of cotton		1.16		.94		2.26
in output		(10.5)		(5.4)		(6.7)
R^2	.311	.473	.474	.54	.373	.691
N	367	367	211	211	49	49

Note: Figures in parentheses (in table body) are t-ratios.

TABLE A.4 Cobb-Douglas production functions, 1860
(Southwest by slaveholding class)

	1–15 SLAVES		16–50 SLAVES		OVER 50 SLAVES	
	(1)	(2)	(3)	(4)	(5)	(6)
Constant	2.45	1.81	2.52	1.77	5.95	1.73
	(5.1)	(4.5)	(4.3)	(3.6)	(3.6)	(1.2)
Value of implements	.143	.120	.203	.145	.103	.136
and machinery	(3.5)	(3.5)	(4.1)	(3.5)	(1.1)	(1.8)
Value of improved	.439	.428	.378	.378	.101	.400
acreage	(6.6)	(7.6)	(5.2)	(6.3)	(0.5)	(2.6)
Free males	.008	.001	-.169	-.041	.074	.057
	(0.1)	(0.0)	(2.3)	(0.7)	(0.5)	(0.5)
Slave males	.171	.155	.202	.153	.432	.096
	(2.5)	(2.7)	(2.4)	(2.1)	(1.8)	(0.5)
Slave females	.132	.102	.385	.272	.042	.098
	(1.8)	(1.7)	(4.0)	(3.4)	(0.1)	(0.4)
Share of cotton in		1.40		1.78		2.09
output		(14.6)		(12.3)		(6.8)
R^2	.246	.473	.356	.558	.244	.548
N	500	500	342	342	74	74

Note: Figures in parentheses (in table body) are t-ratios.

TABLE A.5 Cobb-Douglas production functions, 1850
(Southeast by slaveholding class)

	1–15 SLAVES		16–50 SLAVES	
	(1)	(2)	(3)	(4)
Constant	1.25	1.21	4.23	3.56
	(2.6)	(3.0)	(5.4)	(5.0)
Value of implements and machinery	.174	.138	.011	.123
	(3.8)	(3.6)	(0.1)	(1.2)
Value of improved acreage	.648	.600	.261	.206
	(8.8)	(9.4)	(2.8)	(2.5)
Free males	-.124	-.034	.025	-.012
	(1.4)	(0.4)	(0.2)	(0.1)
Slave males	.152	.050	.222	.102
	(2.0)	(0.8)	(1.4)	(0.7)
Slave females	.082	.084	.504	.394
	(1.0)	(1.2)	(2.7)	(2.4)
Share of cotton in output		1.07		1.55
		(6.2)		(3.9)
R^2	.734	.818	.569	.684
N	90	90	49	49

Note: The Foust sample has less than ten observations of southeastern farms with more than fifty slaves. Figures in parentheses (in table body) are t-ratios.

TABLE A.6 Cobb-Douglas production functions, 1850
(Southwest by slaveholding class)

	1–15 SLAVES		16–50 SLAVES		OVER 50 SLAVES	
	(1)	(2)	(3)	(4)	(5)	(6)
Constant	3.47	3.93	3.14	3.91	2.40	1.39
	(8.7)	(11.2)	(4.2)	(6.8)	(1.1)	(1.2)
Value of implements	.128	.108	.122	.109	.353	.138
and machinery	(2.7)	(2.6)	(2.5)	(2.9)	(2.4)	(1.7)
Value of improved	.387	.256	.350	.195	.484	.519
acreage	(5.7)	(4.1)	(3.1)	(2.2)	(2.0)	(4.0)
Free males	-.028	.030	.075	.042	-.371	-.227
	(0.3)	(0.4)	(0.8)	(0.6)	(1.9)	(2.1)
Slave males	.084	.100	.255	.168	-.285	-.091
	(1.0)	(1.3)	(2.4)	(2.1)	(0.7)	(0.4)
Slave females	.397	.310	.440	.276	.341	.192
	(4.3)	(3.8)	(3.8)	(3.1)	(0.8)	(0.8)
Share of cotton in		1.11		1.64		2.86
output		(6.6)		(8.5)		(9.3)
R^2	.507	.631	.527	.728	.287	.803
N	137	137	105	105	40	40

Note: Figures in parentheses (in table body) are t-ratios.

WORKS CITED

Acemoglu, Daron, Simon Johnson, and James Robinson. "The Rise of Europe: Atlantic Trade, Institutional Change and Economic Growth." *American Economic Review* 95 (2005): 546–79.

Adams, Sean Patrick. *Old Dominion, Industrial Commonwealth: Coal, Politics, and Economy in Antebellum America.* Baltimore: Johns Hopkins University Press, 2004.

Anderson, Ralph V. "Labor Utilization and Productivity, Diversification and Self-Sufficiency: Southern Plantations, 1800–1840." Ph.D. diss., University of North Carolina, 1974.

Anderson, Ralph V., and Robert E. Gallman. "Slaves as Fixed Capital: Slave Labor and Southern Economic Development." *Journal of American History* 64 (June 1977): 24–46.

Angle, Paul M., ed. *Created Equal? The Complete Lincoln-Douglas Debates of 1858.* Chicago: University of Chicago Press, 1958.

Aron, Stephen. *How the West Was Lost: The Transformation of Kentucky from Daniel Boone to Henry Clay.* Baltimore: Johns Hopkins University Press, 1996.

Atack, Jeremy, and Peter Passell. *A New Economic View of American History.* 2nd ed. New York: W.W. Norton, 1994.

Bailyn, Bernard. *The Peopling of British North America: An Introduction.* New York: Vintage Books, 1986.

Baker, O. E. "A Graphic Summary of Seasonal Work on Farm Crops." *Yearbook of the Department of Agriculture* (1917): 537–55.

Bateman-Foust sample. Accessible through the Inter-University Consortium for Political and Social Research, Ann Arbor, MI.

Beckles, Hilary, and Andrew Downes. "The Economics of Transition to the Black Labor System in Barbados: 1630–1680." *Journal of Interdisciplinary History* 18 (1987): 225–47.

Berlin, Ira. *Many Thousands Gone.* Cambridge, MA: Belknap Press, 1998.

Berlin, Ira, and Philip D. Morgan, eds. *Cultivation and Culture: Labor and the Shaping of Slave Life in the Americas.* Charlottesville: University Press of Virginia, 1993.

———, eds. *The Slaves' Economy: Independent Production by Slaves in the Americas.* London: Frank Cass, 1991.

Bezis-Selfa, John. *Forging America: Ironworkers, Adventurers, and the Industrious Revolution.* Ithaca, NY: Cornell University Press, 2004.

———. "A Tale of Two Ironworks: Slavery, Free Labor, Work, and Resistance in the Early Republic." *William and Mary Quarterly.* 3rd ser. 56 (1999): 677–700.

Blackburn, Robin. *The Making of New World Slavery.* London: Verso, 1997.

———. "The Old World Background to European Colonial Slavery." *William and Mary Quarterly* 54 (January 1997): 65–102.

———. *The Overthrow of Colonial Slavery, 1776–1848.* London: Verso, 1988.

Bodenhorn, Howard, and Hugh Rockoff. "Regional Interest Rates in Antebellum America." In *Strategic Factors in Nineteenth Century American Economic History,* edited by Claudia Goldin and Hugh Rockoff, 159–87. Chicago: University of Chicago Press, 1992.

Bolton, Charles C. *Poor Whites of the Antebellum South: Tenants and Laborers in Central North Carolina and Northeast Mississippi.* Durham: Duke University Press, 1994.

Bradshaw, Herbert Clarence. *History of Prince Edward County, Virginia: From Its Earliest Settlements through Its Establishment in 1754 to Its Bicentennial Year.* Richmond, VA: Dietz Press, 1955.

Breen, T. H. *The Marketplace of Revolution: How Consumer Politics Shaped American Independence.* Oxford: Oxford University Press, 2004.

Brody, David. "Free Labor, Law, and American Trade Unionism." In Engerman, *Terms of Labor,* 213–44.

Bruchey, Stuart, ed. *Cotton and the Growth of the American Economy: 1790–1860; Sources and Readings.* New York: Harcourt, Brace and World, 1967.

Bruns, Roger, ed. *Am I Not a Man and a Brother: The Antislavery Crusades of Revolutionary America, 1688–1788.* New York: Chelsea House, 1977.

Burnard, T. G. "'Prodigious Riches': The Wealth of Jamaica before the American Revolution." *Economic History Review* 54 (August 2001): 506–24.

Bushman, Claudia. *In Old Virginia: Slavery, Farming, and Society in the Journal of John Walker.* Baltimore: Johns Hopkins University Press, 2002.

Campbell, John Douglas. "The Gender Division of Labor, Slave Reproduction, and the Slave Family Economy on Southern Cotton Plantations, 1800–1865." Ph.D. diss., University of Minnesota, 1988.

Carlton, David L. *Mill and Town in South Carolina, 1880–1920.* Baton Rouge: Louisiana State University Press, 1982.

Carr, Lois Green, and Russell R. Menard. "Land, Labor, and Economies of Scale in Early Maryland: Some Limits to Growth in the Chesapeake System of Husbandry." *Journal of Economic History* 44 (June 1989): 407–18.

Carrington, Selwyn H. H. *The Sugar Industry and the Abolition of the Slave Trade, 1775.* Gainesville: University Press of Florida, 2002.

Chaplin, Joyce E. *An Anxious Pursuit: Agricultural Innovation and Modernity in the Lower South, 1730–1815.* Chapel Hill: University of North Carolina Press, 1993.

Cloud, Patricia, and David W. Galenson. "Chinese Immigration and Contract Labor in the Late Nineteenth Century." *Explorations in Economic History* 24 (1987): 22–42.

Coats, A. W. "Changing Attitudes to Labour in the Mid-Eighteenth Century." *Economic History Review* 11 (1958): 35–51.

Cobb, James C. *The Most Southern Place on Earth: The Mississippi Delta and the Roots of Regional Identity.* New York: Oxford University Press, 1992.

Coclanis, Peter. "How the Low Country Was Taken to Task." In *Slavery, Secession, and Southern History,* edited by Robert Louis Paquette and Louis A Ferleger, 59–78. Charlottesville: University Press of Virginia, 2000.

———. "The Wealth of British America on the Eve of the Revolution." *Journal of Interdisciplinary History* 21 (Autumn 1990): 245–60.

Coelho, Philip R., and Robert A. McGuire. "African and European Bound Labor in the New World." *Journal of Economic History* 57 (1997): 83–115.

Cohn, David. *Where I Was Born and Raised.* Notre Dame: University of Notre Dame Press, 1967. First published 1948.

Connolly, Michelle. "Human Capital and Growth in the Postbellum South: A Separate but Unequal Story." *Journal of Economic History* 64 (2004): 363–99.

Conrad, Alfred H., and John R. Meyer. "The Economics of Slavery in the Ante-Bellum South." *Journal of Political Economy* 66 (1958): 95–122.

Cornelius, Janet Duitsman. *"When I Can Read My Title Clear": Literacy, Slavery, and Religion in the Antebellum South.* Columbia: University of South Carolina Press, 1991.

Covert, James R. *Seedtime and Harvest.* For U.S. Department of Agriculture, *Bureau of Statistics Bulletin 85.* Washington, DC, 1912.

Crouzet, Francois. "America and the Crisis of the British Imperial Economy, 1803–1807." In McCusker and Morgan, *The Early Modern Atlantic Economy,* 278–315.

Curtin, Philip D. *The Rise and Fall of the Plantation Complex.* New York: Cambridge University Press, 1990.

Darity, William A. "A General Equilibrium Model of the Eighteenth-Century Atlantic Slave Trade." In *Research in Economic History,* edited by Paul Uselding, 7. Greenwich, CT: JAI Press, 1982.

Davis, David B. "American Slavery and the American Revolution." In *Slavery and Freedom in the Age of the Revolution,* edited by Ira Berlin and Ronald Hoffman. Charlottesville: University Press of Virginia, 1983.

———. *The Problem of Slavery in Western Culture.* Ithaca, NY: Cornell University Press, 1966.

———. *Slavery and Human Progress.* New York: Oxford University Press, 1984.

Davis, Thomas J. "Emancipation Rhetoric, Natural Rights, and Revolutionary New England: A Note on Four Black Petitions in Massachusetts, 1773–1777." *New England Quarterly* 62 (1989): 248–63.

DeBow, J. D. B. *Statistical View of the United States: Being a Compendium of the Seventh Census.* Washington, DC: Government Printing Office, 1854.

Decker, Leslie E. "The Great Speculation: An Interpretation of Mid-Continent Pioneering." In *The Frontier in American Development,* edited by David M. Ellis. Ithaca, NY: Cornell University Press, 1969.

Dew, Charles B. *Bond of Iron: Master and Slave at Buffalo Forge.* New York: W. W. Norton, 1994.

———. "Disciplining Slave Ironworkers in the Antebellum South: Coercion, Conciliation, and Accommodation." *American Historical Review* 79 (1974): 393–418.

Donnell, Ezekiel J. *Chronological and Statistical History of Cotton.* New York: J. Sutton, 1872.

Drescher, Seymour. *Capitalism and Antislavery.* New York: Oxford University Press, 1987.

———. *Econocide: British Slavery in the Era of Abolition.* Pittsburgh: University of Pittsburgh Press, 1977.

———. *The Mighty Experiment: Free Labor versus Slavery in British Emancipation.* New York: Oxford University Press, 2002.

———. "White Atlantic?" In Eltis, Lewis, and Sokoloff, *Slavery in the Development of the Americas,* 39.

Dunn, Richard. "'Dreadful' Idlers in the Cane Fields: The Slave Labor Pattern on a Jamaican Sugar Estate, 1762–1831." In *British Capitalism and Caribbean Slavery,* 163–90.

———. *Sugar and Slaves.* Chapel Hill: University of North Carolina Press, 1972.

Earle, Carville. *Geographical Inquiry and American Historical Problems.* Stanford: Stanford University Press, 1992.

Earle, Carville, and Ronald Hoffman. "Staple Crops and Urban Development in the Eighteenth-Century South." *Perspectives in American History* 10 (1976): 5–78. Reprinted in Earle, *Geographical Inquiry and American Historical Problems.*

Edwards, Michael M. *The Growth of the British Cotton Trade, 1780–1815.* Manchester: Manchester University Press, 1967.

Eltis, David, ed. *Coerced and Free Migration: Global Perspectives.* Stanford: Stanford University Press, 2002.

———. *Economic Growth and the Ending of the Transatlantic Slave Trade.* New York: Oxford University Press, 1987.

———. *The Rise of African Slavery in the Americas.* Cambridge: Cambridge University Press, 2000.

Eltis, David, Frank D. Lewis, and Kenneth L. Sokoloff, eds. *Slavery in the Development of the Americas.* New York: Cambridge University Press, 2004.

Engerman, Stanley L. "France, Britain and the Economic Growth of Colonial North America." In McCusker and Morgan, *The Early Modern Atlantic Economy,* 227–49.

———, ed. *Terms of Labor: Slavery, Serfdom, and Free Labor.* Stanford: Stanford University Press, 1999.

Engerman, Stanley L., and Kenneth L. Sokoloff. "The Evolution of Suffrage Institutions in the Americas." *Journal of Economic History* 65 (2005): 891–921.

———. "Factor Endowments, Institutions, and Different Paths of Growth among New World Economies." In *How Latin America Fell Behind,* edited by Stephen Haber, 260–304. Stanford: Stanford University Press, 1997.

Erickson, Charlotte. "Why Did Contract Labor Not Work in the Nineteenth Century United States?" in *International Labour Migration, Historical Perspectives,* edited by Shula Marks and Peter Richardson, 24:34-56. London: Maurice Temple Smith, 1984.

Farmer, Charles J. *In the Absence of Towns.* Lanham, MD: Rowan and Littlefield, 1993.

Fenoaltea, Stefano. "Slavery and Supervision in Comparative Perspective: A Model." *Journal of Economic History* 44 (September 1984): 635–68.

Field-Hendrey, Elizabeth. "Application of a Stochastic Production Frontier to Slave Agriculture: An Extension." *Applied Economics* 27 (1995): 363–68.

Field-Hendrey, Elizabeth, and Lee A. Craig. "The Relative Efficiency of Free and Slave Agriculture in the Antebellum United States: A Stochastic Frontier Approach." In Eltis, Lewis, and Sokoloff, *Slavery in the Development of the Americas,* 236–57.

Findlay, Ronald. *The "Triangular Trade" and the Atlantic Economy of the Eighteenth Century: A Simple General-Equilibrium Model.* Essays in International Finance. Princeton, NJ: International Finance Section, Princeton University, 1990.

Finkelman, Paul. "The Centrality of Slavery in American Legal Development." In *Slavery and the Law*, 3–26.

———. "Evading the Ordinance: The Persistence of Bondage in Indiana and Illinois." *Journal of the Early Republic* 9 (Spring 1989): 21–51.

———. "Slavery and the Constitutional Convention." In *Beyond Confederation*, edited by Richard Beeman, Stephen Botein, and Edward C. Carter III, 189–220. Chapel Hill: University of North Carolina Press, 1987.

———, ed. *Slavery and the Law*. Madison: Madison House Publishers, 1997.

———. "Slavery and the Northwest Ordinance: A Study in Ambiguity." *Journal of the Early Republic* 6 (Winter 1986): 343–70.

———. "Slaves as Fellow Servants: Ideology, Law, and Industrialization." *American Journal of Legal History* 31 (1987): 269–305.

Fleisig, Heywood. "Slavery, the Supply of Agricultural Labor, and the Industrialization of the South." *Journal of Economic History* 36 (1976): 572–97.

Fogel, Robert W. *The Slavery Debates: A Retrospective, 1952–1990*. Baton Rouge: Louisiana State University Press, 2003.

———. *Without Consent or Contract*. New York: W. W. Norton, 1989.

———. *Without Consent or Contract: Technical Papers*. 2 vols. New York: W. W. Norton, 1992.

Fogel, Robert W., and Stanley L. Engerman. "The Economics of Slavery." In *The Reinterpretation of American Economic History*, edited by Robert W. Fogel and Stanley L. Engerman, 311–41. New York: Harper and Row, 1972.

———. "Explaining the Relative Efficiency of Slave Agriculture in the Antebellum South." *American Economic Review* 67 (1977): 275–96.

———. "Explaining the Relative Efficiency of Slave Agriculture in the Antebellum South: Reply." *American Economic Review* 70 (1980): 672–90.

———. *Time on the Cross: The Economics of American Negro Slavery*. 2 vols. Boston: Little, Brown, 1974.

Fogel, Robert W., Ralph A. Galantine, and Richard L. Manning, eds. *Without Consent or Contract: Evidence and Methods*. New York: W.W. Norton, 1992.

Fox-Genovese, Elizabeth, and Eugene D. Genovese. *Fruits of Merchant Capital*. New York: Oxford University Press, 1983.

Galenson, David. "Economic Aspects of the Growth of Slavery in the Seventeenth Century Chesapeake." In Solow, *Slavery and the Rise of the Atlantic System*, 265–92.

———. "The Settlement and Growth of the Colonies." In *The Cambridge Economic History of the United States*. Vol. 1, *The Colonial Era*, edited by Stanley L. Engerman and Robert E. Gallman, 135–207. New York: Cambridge University Press, 1996.

———. *White Servitude in Colonial America.* New York: Cambridge University Press, 1981.

Gaspar, David Barry. "'Rigid and Inclement' Origins of the Jamaica Slave Laws of the Seventeenth Century." In *The Many Legalities of Early America,* edited by Christopher L. Tomlins and Bruce H. Mann, 78–96. Chapel Hill: University of North Carolina Press, 2001.

Genovese, Eugene D. *The Political Economy of Slavery.* New York: Vintage Books, 1965.

———. *Roll, Jordan, Roll: The World the Slaves Made.* New York: Pantheon, 1974.

Glickstein, Jonathan A. "Poverty Is Not Slavery: American Abolitionists and the Competitive Labor Market." In *Antislavery Reconsidered,* edited by Lewis Perry and Michael Fellman, 200–220. Baton Rouge: Louisiana State University Press, 1979.

Grabowski, Richard, and Carl Pasurka. "The Relative Efficiency of Slave Agriculture: An Application of a Stochastic Frontier." *Applied Economics* 21 (1989): 587–95.

Graham, Richard. "Slavery and Economic Development: Brazil and the United States South in the Nineteenth Century." *Comparative Studies in Society and History* 23 (1981): 620–55.

Gray, Lewis Cecil. *History of Agriculture in the Southern United States to 1860.* Washington, DC: Carnegie Institution of Washington, 1933.

Greene, Jack P. *Pursuits of Happiness: The Social Development of Early Modern British Colonies and the Formation of American Culture.* Chapel Hill: University of North Carolina Press, 1988.

Griffiths, Trevor, Philip A. Hunt, and Patrick K. O'Brien. "Inventive Activity in the British Textile Industry, 1700–1800." *Journal of Economic History* 52 (December 1992): 881–906.

Guasco, Suzanne Cooper. "'The Deadly Influence of Negro Capitalists': Southern Yeomen and the Resistance to the Expansion of Slavery in Illinois." *Civil War History* 47 (March 2001): 7–29.

Hammond, Matthew B. *The Cotton Industry: An Essay in American Economic History.* New York: Johnson Reprint Corporation, 1966. First published 1897.

Hancock, David. "'A Revolution in the Trade:' Wine Distribution and the Development of the Infrastructure of the Atlantic Market Economy, 1703–1807." In McCusker and Morgan, *The Early Modern Atlantic Economy,* 105–53.

Hanes, Christopher. "Turnover Cost and the Distribution of Slave Labor in Anglo-America." *Journal of Economic History* 56 (June 1996): 307–29.

Harris, N. Dwight. *The History of Negro Servitude in Illinois and of the Slavery Agitation in That State.* Chicago: McClurg, 1904.

Harrison, Lowell H. *Kentucky's Road to Statehood*. Lexington: University Press of Kentucky, 1992.

Helms, Douglas. "Soil and Southern History." *Agricultural History* 74 (Fall 2000): 723–58.

Higginbotham, A. Leon, Jr. *In the Matter of Color: Race and the American Legal Process*. New York: Oxford University Press, 1978.

Higginbotham, A. Leon, Jr., and Barbara Kopytoff. "Property First, Humanity Second." *Ohio State Law Journal* 50 (1989): 511–40.

Higman, B. W. *Montpelier, Jamaica: A Plantation Community in Slavery and Freedom, 1739–1912*. Kingston, Jamaica: University of the West Indies Press, 1998.

———. *Slave Population and Economy in Jamaica, 1807–1834*. Cambridge: Cambridge University Press, 1976.

Hodges, Graham Russell. *New York City Cartmen, 1667–1850*. New York: New York University Press, 1986.

Hoffer, Peter Charles. *The Great New York Conspiracy of 1741: Slavery, Crime, and Colonial Law*. Lawrence: University Press of Kansas, 2003.

Hofler, Richard A., and Sherman T. Folland. "The Relative Efficiency of Slave Agriculture: A Comment." *Applied Economics* 23 (1991): 861–68.

Hofstra, Warren R., and Robert D. Mitchell. "Town and Country in Backcountry Virginia." *Journal of Southern History* 59 (1993): 619–46.

Huston, James L. *Calculating the Value of the Union: Slavery, Property Rights, and the Economic Origins of the Civil War*. Chapel Hill: University of North Carolina Press, 2003.

Hutchinson, William T. *Cyrus Hall McCormick: Seed-Time, 1809–1856*. New York: Century, 1930.

Inikori, Joseph E. *Africans and the Industrial Revolution in England: A Study in International Trade and Economic Development*. Cambridge: Cambridge University Press, 2002.

Irwin, James. "Exploring the Affinity of Wheat and Slavery in the Virginia Piedmont." *Explorations in Economic History* 25 (Fall 1988): 295–322.

———. "Slave Agriculture and Staple Crops in the Virginia Piedmont." Ph.D. diss., University of Rochester, 1986.

Johnson, Walter. *Soul by Soul: Life inside the Antebellum Slave Market*. Cambridge, MA: Harvard University Press, 1999.

Jones, Alice Hanson. *American Colonial Wealth: Documents and Methods*. Vol. 3. New York: Arno Press, 1977.

———. *Wealth of a Nation to Be: The American Colonies on the Eve of the Revolution*. New York: Columbia University Press, 1980.

Jordan, Winthrop D. *White over Black: American Attitudes toward the Negro, 1550–1812.* Chapel Hill: University of North Carolina Press, 1968.

Kaestle, Carl F. *Pillars of the Republic: Common Schools and American Society, 1780–1860.* New York: Hill and Wang, 1983.

Karsten, Peter. "'Bottomed on Justice': A Reappraisal of Critical Legal Studies Scholarship Concerning Breaches of Labor Contracts by Quitting or Firing in Britain and the U.S., 1630–1880." *American Journal of Legal History* 34 (1990): 213–61.

———. *Heart versus Head: Judge-Made Law in Nineteenth-Century America.* Chapel Hill: University of North Carolina Press, 1997.

Keller, Kenneth. "The Wheat Trade on the Upper Potomac." In Koons and Hofstra, *After the Backcountry,* 21–33.

Kilbourne, Richard Holcombe, Jr. *Debt, Investment, Slaves: Credit Relations in East Feliciana Parish, Louisiana, 1825–1885.* Tuscaloosa: University of Alabama Press, 1995.

King, Alvy L. *Louis T. Wigfall: Southern Fire-eater.* Baton Rouge: Louisiana State University Press, 1970.

Klein, Rachel N. *Unification of a Slave State: The Rise of the Planter Class in the South Carolina Backcountry, 1760–1808.* Chapel Hill: University of North Carolina Press, 1990.

Koons, Kenneth E., and Warren E. Hofstra, eds. *After the Backcountry: Rural Life in the Great Valley of Virginia, 1800–1900.* Knoxville: University of Tennessee Press, 2000.

Kousser, J. Morgan. *The Shaping of Southern Politics: Suffrage Restriction and the Establishment of the One-Party South, 1880–1910.* New Haven, CT: Yale University Press, 1974.

Kulikoff, Allan. *Tobacco and Slaves.* Chapel Hill: University of North Carolina Press, 1986.

Kupperman, Karen Ordahl. "Fear of Hot Climates in the Anglo-American Colonial Experience." *William and Mary Quarterly* 41 (April 1984): 213–39.

Labaree, Leonard W., ed. *The Papers of Benjamin Franklin.* Vol. 9. New Haven, CT: Yale University Press, 1966.

Lakwete, Angela. *Inventing the Cotton Gin: Machine and Myth in Antebellum America.* Baltimore: Johns Hopkins University Press, 2003.

Lebergott, Stanley. "The Demand for Land: The United States, 1820–1860." *Journal of Economic History* 45 (June 1985): 181–212.

———. "'O Pioneers': Land Speculation and the Growth of the Midwest." In *Essays on the Economy of the Old Northwest,* edited by David C. Klingaman and Richard K. Vedder, 37–57. Athens: Ohio University Press, 1987.

Lewis, Ronald L. *Coal, Iron, and Slaves: Industrial Slavery in Maryland and Virginia, 1715–1865*. Westport, CT: Greenwood Press, 1979.

Lindert, Peter H. "Long-Run Trends in American Farmland Values." *Agricultural History* 62 (Summer 1988): 42–82.

Lynd, Staughton. *Class Conflict, Slavery, and the U.S. Constitution*. Indianapolis, IN: Bobbs-Merrill, 1968.

Macleod, Christine. "Strategies for Innovation." *Economic History Review* 45 (1992): 286–304.

Madison, James. *Notes of Debates in the Federal Convention of 1787*. New York: W.W. Norton, 1966. First published 1840.

Main, Gloria. *Tobacco Colony: Life in Early Maryland, 1650–1720*. Princeton, NJ: Princeton University Press, 1982.

Majewski, John. *A House Dividing: Economic Development in Pennsylvania and Virginia before the Civil War*. Cambridge: Cambridge University Press, 2000.

Mancall, Peter, Joshua L. Rosenbloom, and Thomas Weiss. "Agricultural Labor Productivity in the Lower South, 1720–1800." *Explorations in Economic History* 39 (October 2002): 390–424.

Margo, Robert A. *Race and Schooling in the South, 1880–1950: An Economic History*. Chicago: University of Chicago Press, 1990.

Mason, Matthew E. "Slavery Overshadowed: Congress Debates Prohibiting the Atlantic Slave Trade to the United States, 1806–1807." *Journal of the Early Republic* 20 (Spring 2000): 59–81.

McCay, C. F. "The Cultivation of Cotton." in *Eighty Years Progress in the United States*. New York: L. Stebbins, 1864.

McClelland, Peter, and Richard Zeckhauser. *Demographic Dimensions of the New Republic*. Cambridge: Cambridge University Press, 1982.

McCusker, John J., and Russell R. Menard. *The Economy of British America, 1607–1789*. Chapel Hill: University of North Carolina Press, 1985.

McCusker, John J., and Kenneth Morgan, eds. *The Early Modern Atlantic Economy*. Cambridge, MA: Harvard University Press, 2000.

McDougle, Ivan E. *Slavery in Kentucky, 1792–1865*. Lancaster, PA: New Era, 1918.

Meinig, D. W. *The Shaping of America: A Geographical Perspective on Five Hundred Years of History*. Vol. 1, *Atlantic America, 1492–1800*. New Haven, CT: Yale University Press, 1986.

Melish, Joanne Pope. *Disowning Slavery: Gradual Emancipation and "Race" in New England, 1760–1860*. Ithaca, NY: Cornell University Press, 1998.

Menard, Russell R. "The Africanization of the Lowcountry Labor Force." In *Race and Family in the Colonial South*, edited by Winthrop D. Jordan and Sheila L. Skemp, 84–100. Jackson, MS: University Press of Mississippi.

———. "From Servants to Slaves: The Transformation of the Chesapeake Labor System." *Southern Studies* 16 (1977): 355–90.

———. "Slavery, Economic Growth, and Revolutionary Ideology in the South Carolina Lowcountry." In *The Economy of Early America,* edited by Ronald Hoffman, John McCusker, Russell Menard, and Peter J. Albert, 244–74. Charlottesville: University Press of Virginia, 1988.

Metzer, Jacob. "Rational Management, Modern Business Practices, and Economies of Scale in the Ante-Bellum Southern Plantations." *Explorations in Economic History* 12 (April 1975): 123–50.

Miller, Steven F. "Plantation Labor Organization and Slave Life on the Cotton Frontier: The Alabama-Mississippi Black Belt, 1815–1840." In Berlin and Morgan, *Cultivation and Culture,* 155–69.

Montgomery, David. *Citizen Worker.* Cambridge: Cambridge University Press, 1993.

Moore, John Hebron. *Agriculture in Ante-Bellum Mississippi.* New York: Bookman, 1958.

———. *The Emergence of the Cotton Kingdom in the Old Southwest: Mississippi, 1770–1860.* Baton Rouge: Louisiana State University Press, 1988.

Morgan, Philip D. "The Poor: Slaves in Early America." In *Slavery in the Development of the Americas,* 288–323.

———. "Task and Gang Systems: The Organization of Labor on New World Plantations." In *Work and Labor in Early America,* edited by Stephen Innes, 189–220. Chapel Hill: University of North Carolina Press, 1988.

Morris, Thomas D. *Southern Slavery and the Law, 1619–1860.* Chapel Hill: University of North Carolina Press, 1996.

Morriss, Andrew P. "Exploding Myths: An Empirical and Economic Reassessment of the Rise of Employment-at-Will." *Missouri Law Review* 59 (1994): 679–771.

Murphy, Sharon. "Securing Human Property: Slavery, Life Insurance, and Industrialization in the Upper South." *Journal of the Early Republic* 25 (2005): 615–52.

Nash, Gary B. *The Urban Crucible.* Cambridge, MA: Harvard University Press, 1979.

Newell, Margaret Ellen. *From Dependency to Independence: Economic Revolution in Colonial New England.* Ithaca, NY: Cornell University Press, 1998.

Oakes, James. "The Present Becomes the Past: The Planter Class in the Post-bellum South." In *New Perspectives on Race and Slavery in America,* edited by Robert H. Abzug and Stephen E. Maizlish. Lexington: University Press of Kentucky, 1986.

———. *Slavery and Freedom.* New York: Knopf, 1990.

O'Brien, P. K., and Stanley L. Engerman. "Exports and the Growth of the British Economy from the Glorious Revolution to the Peace of Amiens." In Solow, *Slavery and the Rise of the Atlantic System,* 177–209.

Olmstead, Alan L., and Paul W. Rhode. "The Red Queen and the Hard Reds: Productivity Growth in American Wheat, 1800–1940." *Journal of Economic History* 62 (December 2002): 929–66.

———. "Wait a Cotton Pickin' Minute! A New View of Slave Productivity." Paper presented to annual meeting of the Development of the American Economy program (National Bureau of Economic Research), Cambridge, MA, July 2005.

Olmsted, Frederick Law. *The Slave States.* rev. ed. New York: Capricorn Books, 1959. First published 1856, 1857, 1860.

Olson, Mancur. *The Rise and Decline of Nations: Economic Growth, Stagflation, and Social Rigidities.* New Haven, CT: Yale University Press, 1982.

Onuf, Peter S. *Statehood and Union: A History of the Northwest Ordinance.* Bloomington: Indiana University Press, 1987.

Otto, John Solomon. *The Southern Frontiers, 1607–1860.* Westport, CT: Greenwood Press, 1989.

Outland, Robert B., III. "Slavery, Work, and the Geography of the North Carolina Naval Stores Industry, 1835–1860." *Journal of Southern History* 62 (1996): 27–56.

Pares, Richard. *Yankees and Creoles: The Trade between North America and the West Indies before the American Revolution.* London: Longmans, Green, 1956.

Parker, William N., ed. *The Structure of the Cotton Economy in the Antebellum South.* Baltimore: Waverly Press, 1970. First published as the January 1970 issue of *Agricultural History.*

Parker-Gallman sample. Southern Farms Study, 1860. Accessible through the Inter-University Consortium for Political and Social Research, Ann Arbor, MI.

Peabody, Sue. *"There Are No Slaves in France": The Political Culture of Race and Slavery in the Ancien Regime.* New York: Oxford University Press, 1996.

Perdue, Charles L., Thomas E. Barden, and Robert K. Phillips, eds. *Weevils in the Wheat: Interviews with Virginia Ex-Slaves.* Charlottesville: University Press of Virginia, 1976.

Perman, Michael. *Struggle for Mastery: Disfranchisement in the South, 1888–1908.* Chapel Hill: University of North Carolina Press, 2001.

Pessen, Edward. "How Different from Each Other Were the Antebellum North and South?" *American Historical Review* 85 (1980): 1119–49.

Prados de la Escosura, Leandro. "International Comparisons of Real Product, 1820–1990: An Alternative Data Set." *Explorations in Economic History* 37 (2000): 1–41.

Price, Jacob M. *Capital and Credit in British Overseas Trade: The View from the Chesapeake, 1700–1776.* Cambridge, MA: Harvard University Press, 1980.

———. "Credit in the Slave Trade and Plantation Economies." In Solow, *Slavery and the Rise of the Atlantic System,* 293–339.

Price, Jacob M., and Paul G. E. Clemens. "A Revolution of Scale in Overseas Trade: British Firms in the Chesapeake Trade, 1675–1775." *Journal of Economic History* 47 (March 1987): 1–43.

Prude, Jonathan. *The Coming of Industrial Order: Town and Factory Life in Rural Massachusetts, 1810–1860.* Cambridge: Cambridge University Press, 1983.

Quarles, Benjamin. "Antebellum Free Blacks and the 'Spirit of '76.'" *Journal of Negro History* 61 (1976): 229–42.

Ransom, Roger L., and Richard Sutch. "Capitalists without Capital: The Burden of Slavery and the Impact of Emancipation." *Agricultural History* 62 (Summer 1988): 133–60.

———. "Conflicting Visions: The American Civil War as a Revolutionary Event." *Research in Economic History* 20 (2001): 249–301.

Richardson, David. "Slavery, Trade, and Economic Growth in Eighteenth-Century New England." In Solow, *Slavery and the Rise of the Atlantic System,* 237–64.

Robinson, Armstead. "'Worser Than Jeff Davis': The Coming of Free Labor during the Civil War." In *Essays on the Postbellum Southern Economy,* edited by Thavolia Glymph and John J. Kushma, 11–47. College Station: Texas A&M University Press, 1985.

Romer, Paul M. "Why, Indeed, in America? Theory, History and the Origins of Modern Economic Growth." *American Economic Review* 86 (May 1996): 202–6.

Rosenberg, Morton M., and Denis V. McClurg. *The Politics of Pro-Slavery Sentiment in Indiana, 1816–1861.* Muncie, IN: Ball State University, 1968.

Rothenberg, Winifred. *From Market-Places to a Market Economy.* Chicago: University of Chicago Press, 1992.

Rothman, Adam. *Slave Country: American Expansion and the Origins of the Deep South.* Cambridge, MA: Harvard University Press, 2005.

Rubens, Daniel Adam. "Debating the Policy of Slavery in the Ohio Valley, 1787–1824." Department of History Honors thesis, Stanford University, 2005.

Rubin, Julius. "The Limits of Agricultural Progress in the Nineteenth-Century South." *Agricultural History* 49 (Spring 1975): 362–73.

Russell, Thomas D. "Articles Sell Best Singly: The Disruption of Slave Families at Court Sales." *Utah Law Review* 1161 (1996): 1161–1209.

———. "A New Image of the Slave Auction: An Empirical Look at the Role of Law in Slave Sales and a Conceptual Reevaluation of Slave Property." *Cardozo Law Review* 18 (November 1996): 473–523.

Ryden, David Beck. "Does Decline Make Sense? The West Indian Economy and the Abolition of the British Slave Trade." *Journal of Interdisciplinary History* 31 (Winter 2001): 347–74.

Salinger, Sharon V. "Artisans, Journeymen, and the Transformation of Labor in Late Eighteenth-Century Philadelphia." *William and Mary Quarterly* 40 (January 1983): 62–84.

———. *"To Serve Long and Faithfully": Labor and Indentured Servitude in Pennsylvania, 1682–1800*. Cambridge: Cambridge University Press, 1987.

Savitt, Todd L. "Slave Life Insurance in Virginia and North Carolina." *Journal of Southern History* 43 (1977): 583–600.

Schaefer, Donald F. "The Effect of the 1859 Crop Year upon Relative Productivity in the Antebellum Cotton South." *Journal of Economic History* 43 (1983): 851–65.

———. "A Model of Migration and Wealth Accumulation: Farmers at the Antebellum Southern Frontier." *Explorations in Economic History* 24 (1987): 130–57.

———. "A Statistical Profile of Frontier and New South Migrations, 1850–1860." *Explorations in Economic History* 22 (1985): 563–78.

Schmidt, James D. *Free to Work: Labor Law, Emancipation, and Reconstruction, 1815 1880*. Athens: University of Georgia Press, 1998.

Schob, David E. *Hired Hands and Plowboys: Farm Labor in the Midwest, 1815–1860*. Urbana: University of Illinois Press, 1975.

Schumpeter, Elizabeth Boody. *English Overseas Trade Statistics, 1697–1808*. Oxford: Clarendon Press, 1961.

Schweikart, Larry. *Banking in the American South from the Age of Jackson to Reconstruction*. Baton Rouge: Louisiana State University Press, 1987.

Shepherd, James F., and Gary M. Walton. *Shipping, the Maritime Trade, and the Economic Development of Colonial North America*. Cambridge: Cambridge University Press, 1972.

Shore, Laurence. *Southern Capitalists: The Ideological Leadership of an Elite, 1832–1885*. Chapel Hill: University of North Carolina Press, 1986.

Siegel, Frederick F. *The Roots of Southern Distinctiveness: Tobacco and Society in Danville, Virginia, 1780–1865*. Chapel Hill: University of North Carolina Press, 1987.

Simeone, James. *Democracy and Slavery in Frontier Illinois: The Bottomland Republic*. DeKalb: Northern Illinois University Press, 2000.

Smail, John. *Merchants, Markets and Manufacture: The English Wool Textile Industry in the Eighteenth Century*. New York: St. Martin's Press, 1999.

Smith, Adam. *An Inquiry into the Nature and Causes of the Wealth of Nations*. Vol. 1. Oxford: Clarendon Press, 1976. First published 1776.

Smith, S. D. "British Exports to Colonial North America and the Mercantilist Fallacy." *Business History* 37 (January 1995): 45–63.

Solow, Barbara L. "Capitalism and Slavery in the Exceedingly Long Run." In *British Capitalism and Caribbean Slavery*, 51–77.

———. "Slavery and Colonization." In *Slavery and the Rise of the Atlantic System*, 21–42.

———. *Slavery and the Rise of the Atlantic System.* Cambridge: Cambridge University Press, 1991.

———. "The Transatlantic Slave Trade: A New Census." *William and Mary Quarterly* 58 (2001): 11–14.

Solow, Barbara, and Stanley Engerman, eds. *British Capitalism and Caribbean Slavery.* Cambridge: Cambridge University Press, 1987.

Soltow, Lee, and Edward Stevens. *The Rise of Literacy and the Common School in the United States.* Chicago: University of Chicago Press, 1981.

Stampp, Kenneth M. *The Peculiar Institution.* New York: Vintage Books, 1956.

Stealey, John E. "Slavery and the Western Virginia Salt Industry." *Journal of Negro History* 59 (1974): 105–31.

Steinfeld, Robert J. *The Invention of Free Labor: The Employment Relation in English and American Law and Culture, 1350–1870.* Chapel Hill: University of North Carolina Press, 1991.

Swieringa, Robert P. *Pioneers and Profits: Land Speculation on the Iowa Frontier.* Ames: Iowa State University Press, 1968.

Tadman, Michael. *Speculators and Slaves: Masters, Traders, and Slaves in the Old South.* Madison: University of Wisconsin Press, 1989.

Tallant, Harold D. *Evil Necessity: Slavery and Political Culture in Antebellum Kentucky.* Lexington: University Press of Kentucky, 2003.

Thornbrough, Emma Lou. *The Negro in Indiana before 1900.* Bloomington: Indiana University Press, 1985. First published 1957.

Toman, Jane T. "The Gang System and Comparative Advantage." *Explorations in Economic History* 42 (2005): 310–23.

Trautman, Frederic. "Pennsylvania through a German's Eyes: The Travels of Ludwig Gall, 1819–1820." *Pennsylvania Magazine of History and Biography* 105 (January 1981): 35–63.

Turner, Mary, ed. *From Chattel Slaves to Wage Slaves.* Bloomington: Indiana University Press, 1995.

U.S. Bureau of the Census. *Historical Statistics of the United States.* Washington, DC: Government Printing Office, 1975.

U.S. Bureau of the Census. *Negro Population in the United States, 1790–1915.* Washington, DC: Government Printing Office, 1918.

U.S. Bureau of the Census. *Preliminary Report on the Eighth Census.* Washington, DC: Government Printing Office, 1862.

U.S. Department of Agriculture. *Yearbook of the Department of Agriculture.* Washington, DC: Government Printing Office, 1917.

Wahl, Jennifer. *The Bondsman's Burden: An Economic Analysis of the Common Law of Southern Slavery.* Cambridge: Cambridge University Press, 1998.

Walsh, Lorena S. "Plantation Management in the Chesapeake, 1620–1820." *Journal of History* 49 (June 1989): 393–406.

———. "Slave Life, Slave Society, and Tobacco Production in the Tidewater Chesapeake, 1620–1820." In Berlin and Morgan, *Cultivation and Culture*, 170–99.

Walters, Pamela Barnhouse, David R. James, and Holly J. McCammon. "Citizenship and Public Schools: Accounting for Racial Inequality in Education in the Pre- and Disfranchisement South." *American Sociological Review* 62 (1997): 34–52.

Walton, Gary M. "Sources of Productivity Change in American Colonial Shipping, 1675–1775." *Economic History Review* 20 (1967): 67–78.

Ward, J. R. *British West Indian Slavery, 1750–1834.* Oxford: Clarendon Press, 1988.

———. "The British West Indies in the Age of Abolition, 1748–1815." In *The Oxford History of the British Empire.* Vol. 2, *The Eighteenth Century,* edited by P. J. Marshall, 417–36. Oxford: Oxford University Press, 1998.

Ware, Caroline. *The Early New England Cotton Manufacture.* Boston: Houghton Mifflin, 1931.

Watkins, James L. *King Cotton: A Historical and Statistical Review, 1790 to 1908.* New York: Negro Universities Press, 1969. First published 1908.

Weiman, David. "The Economic Emancipation of the Non-Slaveholding Class." *Journal of Economic History* 45 (1985): 71–93.

———. "The First Land Boom in the Antebellum United States: Was the South Different?" In *Structures and Dynamics of Exploitations.* Studies in Social and Economic History, vol. 5, edited by Erik Aerts et al., 27–39. Louvain: Leuven University Press, 1990.

———. "Peopling the Land by Lottery?" *Journal of Economic History* 51 (December 1991): 835–60.

———. "Staple Crops and Slave Plantations: Alternative Perspectives on Regional Development in the Antebellum Cotton South." In *Agriculture and National Development: Views on the Nineteenth Century,* edited by Louis Ferleger, 119–61. Ames: Iowa State University Press, 1990.

Wiebe, Robert H. *Self-Rule: A Cultural History of American Democracy.* Chicago: University of Chicago Press, 1995.

Williams, Eric. *Capitalism and Slavery.* Chapel Hill: University of North Carolina Press, 1944.

Wood, Betty. *Women's Work, Men's Work: The Informal Slave Economies of Lowcountry Georgia.* Athens: University of Georgia Press, 1995.

Wood, Gordon. *The Radicalism of the American Revolution.* New York: Knopf, 1992.

Wood, Horace Gray, *A Treatise on the Law of Master and Servant.* 1877. Reprint, Buffalo: Hein, 1981.

Wood, Peter H. *Black Majority: Negroes in Colonial South Carolina from 1670 through the Stono Rebellion.* New York: W. W. Norton, 1974.

Wright, Gavin. "Capitalism and Slavery on the Islands." In *British Capitalism and Caribbean Slavery*, 283–302.

———. "The Efficiency of Slavery: Another Interpretation." *American Economic Review* (1979): 219–26.

———. *Old South, New South: Revolutions in the Southern Economy since the Civil War.* 1986. Reprint, Baton Rouge: Louisiana State University Press, 1996.

———. *The Political Economy of the Cotton South: Households, Markets, and Wealth in the Nineteenth Century.* New York: W.W. Norton, 1978.

———. "Prosperity, Progress, and American Slavery." In *Reckoning with Slavery*, edited by Paul A David et al., 302–36. New York: Oxford University Press, 1976.

———. "Slavery and American Agricultural History." *Agricultural History* 77 (Fall 2003): 527–52.

Zahedieh, Nuala. "London and the Colonial Consumer." *Economic History Review* 47 (May 1994): 239–38.

Zeitz, Joshua Michael. "The Missouri Compromise Reconsidered: Antislavery Rhetoric and the Emergence of the Free Labor Synthesis." *Journal of the Early Republic* 20 (Fall 2000): 447–85.

Zilversmit, Arthur. *The First Emancipation: The Abolition of Slavery in the North.* Chicago: University of Chicago Press, 1967.

Zonderman, David A. *Aspirations and Anxieties: New England Workers and the Mechanized Factory System, 1815–1850.* New York: Oxford University Press, 1992.

INDEX

Page numbers in italic refer to figures and tables.